Johnny Speight

THREE PLAYS

IF THERE WEREN'T ANY BLACKS
YOU'D HAVE TO INVENT THEM

THE COMPARTMENT

THE KNACKER'S YARD

OBERON BOOKS
LONDON

This collection first published in 1998 by Oberon Books Ltd. (incorporating Absolute Classics). *If There Weren't Any Blacks You'd Have to Invent Them* first published by Methuen & Co. in 1968.

Oberon Books Ltd.
(incorporating Absolute Classics)
521 Caledonian Road
London   N7 9RH.
Tel: 0171 607 3637 / Fax: 0171 607 3629
e-mail: oberon.books@btinternet.com

British Library Cataloguing-in-Publication Data
A catalogue record for this book is available from the British Library.

ISBN 1 84002 080 6

Cover design: Andrzej Klimowski

Typography: Richard Doust

Printed in Great Britain by Arrowhead Books Ltd., Reading.

Contents

Foreword

One of the most important names in the history of the first 60 years of television, is that of Johnny Speight. He will, of course, and naturally, be best remembered for the creation of Alf Garnett in *Till Death Us Do Part*, a character who changed the face of television comedy across the world. There are few people (and Warren Mitchell made Garnett a real person) whose Christian name alone in a newspaper headline, is enough to tell us who the story is about; Charles criticises farmers! Philip upsets Australians! Alf in trouble with BBC!

But there is more to Johnny Speight than Alf Garnett. His early work included radio scripts for Frankie Howerd and Arthur Askey; on television he wrote nearly 500 episodes of the *Arthur Haynes Show*, and for Morecambe and Wise, and Peter Sellers. He also wrote the first series of a 20-year run of *Sykes*, for his friend Eric. And, of course, *Till Death Us Do Part* and *In Sickness and in Health*.

I've known and worked with Johnny for over 30 years, starting as an assistant floor manager at the BBC. And I've produced and directed much of what he has written for television in the last 20 years; *Spooner's Patch* (with Ray Galton); the award-winning *The Lady is a Tramp* (for Patricia Hayes); *The Nineteenth Hole* (for Eric Sykes) and the return of Alf Garnett to television in the 1980s. It has been a successful and happy relationship, and there is no other writer I'd rather work with.

I cannot explain what goes on in his head as he writes, but I've sat in his study at his home for hours as he banged away on his old typewriter, which he later, to my great surprise, replaced with a word processor!

7

And when he does work it pours out of him. He doesn't worry about typing errors or spelling mistakes, and he does almost no editing or rewriting. He just writes. Sometimes a single thought will take him through two or three pages of dialogue just as fast as he can type. Most of what he writes is pure gold; and it displays an insight into the human mind and human behaviour, and an ear for the way his characters express themselves, that I can only believe to be instinct. He certainly can't have been taught it.

The part of Johnny's work that the millions who love his television writing know little of, is contained in this book. He is a dramatist of distinction and had television not taken so much of his time he would certainly have written more for the theatre. In these three plays you'll find more logical argument, and more common sense than you'll find in most plays. And his rhythms of speech and trains of thought are as close as you'll ever hear to the real thing. They are all, at the same time, provocative, disturbing, and funny. Very funny.

My own favourite is *The Compartment* (in which a young Michael Caine played the lead) but that's a bit like asking who was the greatest boxer in the world Joe Louis, Sugar Ray Robinson or Mohammed Ali. Take your pick – or better still, enjoy them all.

William G. Stewart
London, 1998

IF THERE WEREN'T ANY BLACKS
YOU'D HAVE TO INVENT THEM

If There Weren't Any Blacks You'd Have to Invent Them was first presented by London Weekend Television in August 1968 with the following cast:

SEXTON, Ronald Radd

VICAR, Laurence Hardy

UNDERTAKER, Frank Thornton

PRIVATE, Leonard Cracknell

OFFICER, Moray Watson

ROBIN'S MOTHER, Sally Bowers

MUSICIAN, Peter Craze

BLIND MAN, Leslie Sands

BACKWARDS MAN, Jimmy Hanley

YOUNG MAN, John Castle

PRIEST, Paul Hardwick

DOCTOR, Derek Godfrey

NURSE, Valerie Leon

GIRL, Nerys Hughes

JEWISH MOTHER, Amelia Bayntun

JUDGE, Kynaston Reeves

Directed by Charles Jarrott

PART ONE

Open on funeral: procession moving towards a grave through a Cemetery.

Cut to bell tolling.

Cut to:

SEXTON: I shouldn't have to do this. Not my job. Just the muggins that's all I am. The bloody dogsbody. Got to dig holes ... fill 'em in ... ring bells ... dig more bloody holes ... fill them in. All the others do is chat and give out orders.

We see the VICAR murmuring the funeral service from the SEXTON's point of view.

SEXTON: That bloody Vicar's got it easy he has. All he ever does is pray. Prays for this, prays for the other. I'm too bloody busy to pray I am. (*He stops pulling the rope.*) That'll do. (*He picks up his shovel.*) Got to go an' fill another hole in now.

A VICAR in a surplice is intoning from a book. A kind of service. After a few seconds he comes to the end and shuts his book. This scene should appear as normal and everyday as possible. The VICAR looks at the UNDERTAKER and they both look at the youth, the PRIVATE, then they turn and walk away. The youth stands still staring into the grave. He is now completely alone, head bowed. Another youngish man, the OFFICER, comes from around the back of the vault and stands staring at the youth. He is dressed in guards mufti, bowler, narrow drain pipe trousers, tight fitting hacking style jacket. After a while he puts his hand into his pocket and brings out a revolver. He walks silently over to the youth and places the gun at his head. The youth jumps, startled.

OFFICER: Don't be frightened. I'm not going to hurt you.

PRIVATE: What do you want?

OFFICER: Don't worry. It's quite all right. Just do what I tell you. You'll be all right, don't worry. I've been waiting for you.

PRIVATE: Waiting for ... for me?

OFFICER: Well not exactly, but someone like you. Someone your build. Someone your size.

PRIVATE: My size?

OFFICER: Near enough your size.

PRIVATE: No ... you've made a mistake ... it's not me

OFFICER: Oh no. There's been no mistake. It's you all right. You're the one. Five foot ten, forty-two chest, thirty-one waist ... a bit long in the leg I think, but they'll turn up all right. What's your cap size?

PRIVATE: Cap size?

OFFICER: What cap size do you take?

PRIVATE: I don't know. I never wear a cap.

OFFICER: Try this on. (*He puts his bowler on PRIVATE's head. It fits.*) Ah yes, that's it, That's a good fit. You'll do fine.

PRIVATE: I ... but what ... I don't understand.

OFFICER: Doesn't matter. Just get undressed.

PRIVATE: Undressed ... I ... No ... No ...

OFFICER: Look, you mustn't be insubordinate. This gun's loaded, I suppose you know that?

PRIVATE: Leave me alone. I haven't done you any harm. I don't even know you.

OFFICER: Of course you don't. We haven't even met. But we'll get to know each other. We'll get to know each other quite a lot ... in the future ... you'll see. Now come on, get undressed ...

PRIVATE: No ...

OFFICER: (*Threateningly.*) Get undressed.

PRIVATE: (*Terrified.*) What ... here? Just here?

OFFICER: Behind the vault ... come on ... hurry up.

PRIVATE: No ... I don't want to. I'm not going to ...

OFFICER: Look. Please, don't make me shoot you. It's all right. I'm getting undressed too. There's no need to be shy. (*He presses the gun closer to the PRIVATE's head.*) Look, are you going to get undressed? I'm not going to stand arguing you know. It's not my position to stand here arguing with you. I'm a decent type, but I won't stand insubordination. That's one thing I will not tolerate. I'm a fair-minded man, but I'm also a disciplinarian. Now, either you get undressed or I pull this trigger.

PRIVATE: No, don't shoot ... I ... I ... I'll get undressed.

OFFICER: That's better. Come on, behind the vault ... hurry up.

They both walk behind the vault. The OFFICER with the gun at the PRIVATE's head. As they disappear behind the vault we cut fast to close-up on cymbal being played very fast. Then as the rest of the group come on we pan round to reveal small POP GROUP playing very fast up tempo with tenor taking solo. We pan round still further to reveal a woman in complete and heavy mourning veiled, sitting listening to them. By her side stands the UNDERTAKER. Four GIRLS are dancing to the group.

UNDERTAKER: (*In a respectful tone to the woman.*) They're a fine group.

ROBIN'S MOTHER: Yes ... so I believe.

UNDERTAKER: They're regarded very highly in pop circles.

ROBIN'S MOTHER: It was Robin's favourite band. And he understood this music.

UNDERTAKER: Oh, yes, they're very good.

ROBIN'S MOTHER: Robin wouldn't have liked anything that wasn't of the highest quality.

UNDERTAKER: Robin had taste.

ROBIN'S MOTHER: Impeccable taste.

UNDERTAKER: I think they're an excellent memorial to him.

ROBIN'S MOTHER: Yes, he would have liked it I'm sure. When he was alive he always wanted me to buy this band for him. He had all the records, and the high-fi equipment to play them on, but it wasn't enough for Robin. He was a perfectionist you see. He wanted the band, and I refused him. (*She starts to cry.*) I shall never forgive myself for that ...

UNDERTAKER: You mustn't upset yourself, you did everything for Robin ...

ROBIN'S MOTHER: But not that. I didn't do the one thing he wanted most. I bought him everything else. Position in life ... a beautiful bride ... a house to live in with her, but not the band. The thing he wanted most I refused him. (*She sobs quietly.*) I tried to buy it when he was ill ... when I knew he wouldn't ... wouldn't recover ... I tried then. I fitted a stage ... a complete stage ... into his sick room, and got them to play there for him all day long, but he was too ill then to enjoy it. Even the girls ... his favourite girls, nasty painted-up creatures, but he seemed to find so much pleasure in them. I bought those for him too, but it was all too late. Too late for him to enjoy them. (*Sobs.*) I let him down. I wasn't there when Robin needed me most. Oh Robin, Robin, please forgive me.

UNDERTAKER: He does. I'm sure he does. Now you mustn't upset yourself. You were a good mother to Robin, and he loved you very much, very much.

Cut to: POP GROUP and GIRLS dancing.

Cut to:

SEXTON: (*Still shovelling, talks into the camera.*) Bloody marvellous ain't it, eh? Bloody live memorials to the bloody dead. Dunno what it's all coming to I don't. I mean music in here, pop groups playing here. I mean, it don't seem right do it? It ain't like the old days. Bloody potty she is ... right round the bend.

Cut to: the UNDERTAKER helping up ROBIN'S MOTHER and putting his arm through hers.

UNDERTAKER: Come ... I think you've had enough for today, these memories are too bitter for you. (*He motions the GROUP to stop.*) That's enough, that's enough for now.

The GROUP stop playing and he leads ROBIN'S MOTHER off. As they go the GROUP packs up and they start to put their instruments away. The SEXTON comes on carrying a spade.

SEXTON: (*To the GROUP.*) You finished?

MUSICIAN: Yes, she broke down again.

SEXTON: She won't get over him you know. She's broken hearted she is. She doted on him, on that boy. Give him everything.

MUSICIAN: Well it's done us a favour anyway. It's got us a nice little number.

SEXTON: Yer, oh yer. That's what I always say about it, death, it's a good thing – makes room for others. (*He starts to fill in the grave.*) I wish they'd burn 'em though. Twenty-five I've put down here this week, twenty-five of 'em, two to a hole; that's thirteen holes I've had to dig. They ought to burn 'em, that's what they ought to do with 'em. But it's them religions, they're the ones what's against it, they're the one's against the burning. It's all right for them, though, ain't it? They ain't got to dig the holes have they?

MUSICIAN: Cremation'll make you redundant won't it?

SEXTON: No. I could get a job stoking. Better job that is, specially in the winter. No, all this digging mate, it ain't doing me no good.

MUSICIAN: Yer, well, see you pops ...

They start to move off. The SEXTON carries on with his work. The GROUP move through cemetery and we see two men enter. One is blind with white stick and dark glasses and he is leading by the arm another man who is walking backwards.

BACKWARDS MAN: How are we in front?

BLIND MAN: (*Waving his stick.*) All right I think.

BACKWARDS MAN: No obstacles?

BLIND MAN: (*Waving his stick.*) No ... no obstacles. The way forward seems quite clear.

BACKWARDS MAN: Good. That's the idea, that's great.

BLIND MAN: Where are we?

BACKWARDS MAN: We're passing through a cemetery.

BLIND MAN: What's it like?

BACKWARDS MAN: I don't know.

BLIND MAN: Describe it to me.

BACKWARDS MAN: I can't.

BLIND MAN: Why not?

BACKWARDS MAN: I've shut my eyes.

BLIND MAN: You're always shutting your eyes. Anything you don't like, anything you're afraid to look at you shut your eyes.

BACKWARDS MAN: Why shouldn't I? That's what eyes are for. That's why eyes were made to close. We should use all our facilities. It's no good having shutters on your eyes if you don't use them.

The BLIND MAN waving his stick in front of him comes up against a bench. His stick strikes it and he stops.

BLIND MAN: What's this? (*He taps at it with his stick, then he feels it.*)

BACKWARDS MAN: What is it?

BLIND MAN: It's ... I think it's a seat ... yes it's a bench ... it's a bench of some sort.

BACKWARDS MAN: A bench. (*He feels behind him, trying to feel the bench.*) Hmm ... it is ... I think it is a bench ...

BLIND MAN: Turn around, have a look, see what it is.

BACKWARDS MAN: No, I mustn't face that direction, you know I mustn't. (*Still groping behind at the bench.*) It is a bench, a slatted bench, with no back. It's got no back rest.

BLIND MAN: And slats, it's got slats.

BACKWARDS MAN: It's got slats.

BLIND MAN: Shall we sit on it?

BACKWARDS MAN: Sit on it?

BLIND MAN: Well that's what it's there for ... it's been put there for that reason.

BACKWARDS MAN: But I'm not tired.

BLIND MAN: If you wait till you're tired, there may not be a bench.

BACKWARDS MAN: That's true. They're always in the wrong places, these amenities. Benches in places where you're not tired, drinking fountains in places where you're not thirsty ...

BLIND MAN: We should synchronise our habits. You're never tired when I am, and never thirsty or hungry when I am. It's ridiculous this anarchy. We waste time, stopping twice where we only need to stop once.

BACKWARDS MAN: All right. I'll sit down and rest with you.

They both sit. The BLIND MAN facing one way, the BACKWARDS MAN facing the other.

BACKWARDS MAN: (*Feeling the seat.*) There's a plaque here ...

BLIND MAN: A plaque.

BACKWARDS MAN: On the seat here ...

BLIND MAN: What does it say?

BACKWARDS MAN: I don't know ... I've still got my eyes shut.

BLIND MAN: Well open them and read it. It might be important.

BACKWARDS MAN: No I can't open them yet. You feel it. You've got better touch than I have ... feel the letters.

BLIND MAN: (*Feels on the seat.*) They're very worn.

BACKWARDS MAN: It's not in braille?

BLIND MAN: No. Nothing is ever in braille.

BACKWARDS MAN: People are not fair to the blind. Everything should be in braille, all signs, notices, street names, advertisements on hoardings should be in every language including braille.

BLIND MAN: True, though street names and hoardings would be too high to reach.

BACKWARDS MAN: Then let them get ladders. There's a way round everything if we only had the will.

BLIND MAN: Will ... there's not enough will. You haven't even got the will to keep your eyes open.

BACKWARDS MAN: I've got the will to keep them shut.

The two men re-appear from behind the vault. The one with the gun is now dressed as an ARMY OFFICER and the other one is now dressed as a PRIVATE. The OFFICER still has the gun at the PRIVATE's forehead.

OFFICER: Attention ... quick march ... right wheel ... left wheel ... moving to the left in fours ... moving to the right in fours ... about turn ... left right ... left right ... left ... left ... left right left.

The OFFICER brings out a bugle and blows a march on it as they go off.

BLIND MAN: What's that?

BACKWARDS MAN: It's the military I think ... manoeuvres.

BLIND MAN: A church parade.

BACKWARDS MAN: It's not Sunday.

BLIND MAN: A military funeral ...

BACKWARDS MAN: That's more like it, that's probably it.

A YOUNG MAN walks on and up to the bench. He hesitates before it, looking at the two men. Then he sits down.

YOUNG MAN: Er ... you don't mind if I sit here, do you?

BACKWARDS MAN: No ... not at all.

YOUNG MAN: I don't like sitting with strangers normally, at least not on benches ... public places. It's not that I'm a nervous type. I never have been. I mean even in the old days, when the family used to go away. I was never nervous about being alone in the house. I've always slept on my own anyway. As long as the door is bolted and I can have a light burning I'm not bothered. It's just that I'm not keen on strangers. Well, I mean you don't know them do you? And you hear of so many funny things happening in parks and public places. The authorities are to blame. They should keep them more private, these public places. But they're not bothered, they let anyone into them. I mean you can go into a park and you don't know who you're expected to mix with, and there's some very odd people about. That's why I'm always so careful about talking to strangers. I was brought up that way. My mother, she used always to say to me, if any strangers stop you in the street and offer you sweets be sure not to take them. And I never have. She was a marvellous woman my mother, and I was, very fond of her. Well, she was so good to me. You see when I was young I had these dirty habits, and she house-trained me. She got me clean, completely clean, so that I could go into

people's houses without showing myself up. And
I haven't disgraced myself now, not since I was eight,
eight or nine. I've had no lapses at all since then.
Not one single lapse. Every morning when I wake up,
the bed is as dry and clean as it was when I got into it,
and I don't need rubbers or anything. If she knew she'd
be terribly proud of me I know.

BACKWARDS MAN: Is she dead?

YOUNG MAN: Yes. She died of one of those postal
diseases. It's all the GPO's fault. It's them I blame.
They allow the letters to mix up like that. They let 'em
mingle in those pillar boxes, and you get letters from
clean people mixing up, laying by the side of letters
from dirty people. They shouldn't be allowed to write
letters, people like that. They should be made to have
a medical ... get a clean bill of health before they're
allowed to write letters. They're sending their diseases
through the post. It ought to be stopped. I've had to
change my name I have, and my address, and keep 'em
both secret, so that people can't send me their diseases
in the mail, Er ... if you're not ... er ... I mean you're
clean, are you? You haven't got anything wrong with
you have you?

BACKWARDS MAN: No. My friend is blind, but it's not
contagious.

YOUNG MAN: Oh no. That's one of the good things
about blindness, it's not catching. You see I don't mind
people being ill. I'm quite broad-minded about illness,
as long as it isn't catching, as long as they don't spread
it about. That's another reason why I don't like meeting
strangers, because you can't tell what diseases they
might have. Ladies' gloves you know, they carry
terrible diseases on them, if you put them on I mean.

A chap I know, he told me that ... He said you can catch terrible diseases from putting on ladies' gloves, or any of their clothes, actually. Do you think that's true?

BACKWARDS MAN: I don't know.

BLIND MAN: I've heard tales of men wearing women's clothes, but being blind I've never seen one.

YOUNG MAN: That's some kink isn't it? I mean you'd have to be kinky to do that sort of thing, wouldn't you? Er ... you're not kinky I suppose, you or your friend?

BACKWARDS MAN: No.

YOUNG MAN: Oh good. Only I find it can be very awkward if you're in the company of people who are kinky, not that I have been, because I always make a point of avoiding that type of person, but I imagine it could be very embarrassing.

BACKWARDS MAN: I close my eyes to those sort of things.

BLIND MAN: He closes his eyes to everything.

BACKWARDS MAN: I have to. In the company of the blind one has to be blind. It's our only chance of survival. What's the use of me seeing things you can't see? If we were too different we'd never get on.

BLIND MAN: He believes the blind should lead the blind.

BACKWARDS MAN: It's the only kind of leadership that's tolerable.

YOUNG MAN: Well, I'm a bit out of my depth here. I think, I mean, not having been blind, or political, but I do think we should all try to be as much like our friends as possible, I mean this trying to be different.

It's all very well, isn't it, but I don't think it works, you know. Not in real life. That's why I don't like strangers. I mean, they might be different; you can't tell until the damage is done. I mean, I believe in equality, but it's no good having equality if some people are going to be superior, I mean, we've got to decide what the equal is, and then all stick to it. But some people don't you see. They're always trying to be cleverer. This chap I knew, he was terribly successful, well, he used to get all these marvellous, brilliant ideas you see, millions of them, and he used to get all the credit for them. I mean, that sort of thing isn't fair. Ideas should be shared I think ... don't matter who gets them. Otherwise, it makes some people look better than others.

BLIND MAN: You're not coloured are you?

YOUNG MAN: No.

BLIND MAN: You're sure.

YOUNG MAN: Yes, I'm completely white, all white, all over. If you could see, you would see that I was white. Even underneath.

BLIND MAN: All right. I'll take your word for it. I suppose I'll have to.

YOUNG MAN: But I am white. Really, I'm as white as anybody. I mean, ask your friend. Ask him to have a look. He'll tell you.

BLIND MAN: It's no good asking him to look at anything.

BACKWARDS MAN: I don't want to get involved in any colour question.

YOUNG MAN: But I am white. I'm as white as you are.

BLIND MAN: I've only got your word for that.

YOUNG MAN: But I am.

BLIND MAN: I say you're not.

YOUNG MAN: But I am white.

BLIND MAN: You're not as white as I am. I'm pure white, the purest white, and nobody's whiter.

YOUNG MAN: I didn't say I was whiter ... I said as white.

BLIND MAN: No, no, no. Not as white, not as white, You're nowhere near as white. A bloody liberal that's what you are. One of those bloody damned equalisers. I tell you, I'm whiter than you, much whiter, and I'm blind and you're not, and that makes me much different, much different to you.

BACKWARDS MAN: Oh dear, he's bringing politics into it again. You mustn't argue with my friend on politics, sex or religion. He has certain beliefs and they mustn't be challenged.

YOUNG MAN: But ...

BACKWARDS MAN: Enough. Please don't be offensive.

BLIND MAN: I'm sure he's coloured. He's black, I know it. I knew it as soon as he sat down. I sensed it.

YOUNG MAN: But I'm not.

BACKWARDS MAN: You're arguing again.

YOUNG MAN: But I'm not. I'm just stating facts, that's all.

BACKWARDS MAN: In a very argumentative fashion.

BLIND MAN: He's black. As black as a pot.

YOUNG MAN: I'm not black I tell you. I might wear women's clothes occasionally, and have dirty habits, but I'm not black, that's one thing I'm not.

BACKWARDS MAN: His voice doesn't sound black.

BLIND MAN: It doesn't?

BACKWARDS MAN: It sounds to me, more middle-class English.

BLIND MAN: So that's their bloody game is it? They're learning to speak bloody middle-class English now are they. Hoping that'll hide their colour, eh? Well it won't, it won't, not as far as the blind are concerned anyway.

YOUNG MAN: (*Getting up.*) I'm going. I knew I shouldn't have done it, talking to strangers, they're horrible, they're always horrible. (*Almost to himself.*) You were right Mum, I mustn't talk to strangers, or take sweets off 'em, 'cos they're nasty, they're nasty horrible people. (*He gets up and runs. He stops a few feet away and shouts back almost like a small boy.*) You're black, you're the one what's black, you are, and if you had eyes you'd see it. Old blackie, old blackie.

The YOUNG MAN runs off. The BLIND MAN turns round and grabs the BACKWARDS MAN.

BLIND MAN: I'm not black am I? I'm not. Tell me. He's telling lies, isn't he? I'm white, I'm purest white. Tell me I am, aren't I?

BACKWARDS MAN: I don't know, I can't see you.

BLIND MAN: Open your eyes. Quick look at me. Look at me. Tell me I'm white.

BACKWARDS MAN: I'd rather not. I'd rather not look, just in case.

BLIND MAN: Just in case, you mean, just in case ... I ... might be black.

BACKWARDS MAN: Well, we don't know, do we?

BLIND MAN: Oh God, God. No. I mustn't be. I can't be. I must be white. Look, please look, and reassure me that I'm not ... please ... please ... tell me that I'm white.

BACKWARDS MAN: You're white.

BLIND MAN: Have you looked?

BACKWARDS MAN: No.

BLIND MAN: Look, and then tell me.

BACKWARDS MAN: It's too risky, far too risky. We don't want to destroy our belief in each other. It's better to be what we believe we are, and not look at each other any closer. You're white, you're white, the purest white, and so am I.

BLIND MAN: Yes. I'm white, I'm very, very white, as white as can be.

He murmurs on ad lib: 'White, white, white, white' like a prayer almost inaudible. Then a pause.

BACKWARDS MAN: We've come through a very sticky patch old friend, a very sticky patch.

BLIND MAN: Yes, but we've come through it.

BACKWARDS MAN: With our faith unshaken.

BLIND MAN: With our beliefs unshattered.

BACKWARDS MAN: You see, my philosophy works. What the eyes don't see, the heart don't grieve over. When your beliefs are challenged, just shut your eyes and have faith.

BLIND MAN: Yes. I'll never sneer at it again my friend. It's a great way of life.

BACKWARDS MAN: It's the only way. Besides it makes us so much more equal.

BLIND MAN: What?

BACKWARDS MAN: Me keeping my eyes shut. This way I can be as blind as you are. It rules out the difference.

BLIND MAN: You and your damned equality. Why can't you let me be different?

BACKWARDS MAN: That other chap had the right idea. He said that friends should try to be like each other. That's friendly, very friendly that is ...

BLIND MAN: That damned black.

BACKWARDS MAN: We don't know he was black.

BLIND MAN: I touched his skin, it felt different. It had larger pores, too large for a white skin, far too large.

BACKWARDS MAN: We don't know.

BLIND MAN: Don't talk to me any more. I've had enough conversation for one day, it's unsettled me. I'm putting my card up.

He hangs a large card round his neck reading 'Please Do Not Disturb' then in large print underneath 'Private Keep Away'. We hear the sound of a bugle and drums playing a boy scout march. The OFFICER and PRIVATE march on. The OFFICER still holding the gun and playing the bugle. The PRIVATE is playing a kettle drum. He has a large Union Jack on a flag pole fastened to his belt. They march right across and off. Pan to a signpost with all church signs on. We see a PRIEST and VICAR approaching. They shake hands.

VICAR: Good morning, Father.

PRIEST: Good morning, Vicar. (*He snuffles.*)

VICAR: What's wrong? You don't look too well this morning.

PRIEST: My nose gets so bunged up these days.
I think it's catarrh.

VICAR: Busy this week?

PRIEST: (*Shakes his head.*) No ... had about ten in on
Sunday.

VICAR: Better than me ... eight I had.

PRIEST: Yes, but you get a salary, old chap. My wages
come out of the plate. The pub was full on Saturday
night though. Most of mine were in there.

VICAR: Most of mine too.

PRIEST: There must be some way of drumming up
business you know.

VICAR: Licensed bar?

PRIEST: Bingo in the afternoons?

VICAR: Snooker table?

PRIEST: At least we'd get the crowds ...

A funeral procession enters.

That one of yours or one of mine, I wonder?

VICAR: Don't know. (*Rising.*) I suppose we'd better check.

*As the funeral procession goes we pan to the DOCTOR and
NURSE coming on. The NURSE in uniform is pushing a
hospital trolley loaded with medical equipment. The
DOCTOR is in pinstripes. They stop and the NURSE helps
the DOCTOR on with a white coat. He then takes up a
stethoscope and blows through it. While he is doing this the
NURSE unbuttons her blouse and the DOCTOR puts the
stethoscope to her chest and listens.*

DOCTOR: Testing ... testing ... breathe in ... breathe out ...
in ... out ... in ... out ... testing ... in ... out ... Hm ... They

seem all right. Sterilise those instruments will you Nurse?

The PRIEST walks from behind the tombstones from the direction of the church. A tumbledown ruin at the back of the cemetery.

PRIEST: Good morning, Doctor.

DOCTOR: Good morning, Father.

PRIEST: I haven't seen you in Church these last few months, have I?

DOCTOR: I've been very busy, Father.

PRIEST: You mustn't let business stand in the way of your religion, you know.

DOCTOR: I don't Father, but it's all these new diseases they keep bringing out. Can you take your shirt off, please. Keep your trousers on. We only have a limited knowledge you know, and they are so far in advance, these new diseases, years in front of us doctors.

The PRIEST starts to disrobe. The NURSE takes his cassock and things, then his shirt and vest.

PRIEST: (*Disrobing.*) And I suppose you haven't been to Holy Communion either?

DOCTOR: No, Father.

PRIEST: Tut, tut. It won't do my boy, you know. It doesn't do to shut God out of your life.

DOCTOR: (*With his stethoscope on the PRIEST's chest now.*) I'm sorry Father, it's not that I've intentionally stayed away.

PRIEST: I'm sure you haven't, but nevertheless you haven't been. Nurse, please.

He indicates a small sash. She hands it to him and he slips it over his shoulders. He then mumbles the beginning of confessional. While he does this the DOCTOR knocks on his chest with his fingers tapping, and listens through the stethoscope again.

DOCTOR: Please, Father, give me your blessing for I have sinned. It is six months since my last confession, and I accuse myself of ... (*All the while still examining PRIEST's chest.*) I have told lies. I have used bad language. I have had bad thoughts ...

PRIEST: Bad thoughts ... about women?

DOCTOR: Yes, Father.

PRIEST: (*Disappointed.*) Ah. (*Pressing on.*) Do you indulge these bad thoughts, my boy?

DOCTOR: No, Father.

PRIEST: Good. You must try and resist them.

DOCTOR: For these and all my other sins which I cannot now remember I humbly ask penance and absolution of you, Father.

The PRIEST starts to murmur confession.

PRIEST: May the passion of our Lord Jesus Christ, the merits of the blessed Virgin Mary, and of all the Saints, whatever good you do, whatever evil you suffer, gain for you a remission of your sins, an increase of grace and the reward of eternal life, amen.

DOCTOR: Hm ... this chest is very congested, very congested. Are you bothered with a cough at all, Father?

PRIEST: Yes, Doctor. (*He goes on murmuring.*) Mostly in the morning. I wake up coughing and with lack of appetite. I thought it was catarrh. For penance I want you to say three Hail Father's and two Hail Mary's.

DOCTOR: Hm. It probably is catarrh. (*Now writing.*) Now I want you to take these three times a day, with water, and I want you to rub the ointment on your chest every night before you go to bed.

PRIEST: Thank you, Doctor. (*He starts to put on his shirt and robes, helped by the NURSE.*) Holy Communion is from eight in the mornings, and try to avoid the bad thoughts my boy.

DOCTOR: Yes Father, and surgery hours are from nine to eleven, and look after that chest. You're not as young now as you used to be. Keep yourself well wrapped up. We don't want you to be taken from us.

PRIEST: When the Maker calls I shall be ready.

DOCTOR: Ah yes, but there's no need to go before then.

The PRIEST walks off, reading his book. The YOUNG MAN appears. The DOCTOR sees him.

DOCTOR: Shirt off.

YOUNG MAN: Sssh, those two blacks haven't gone yet.

DOCTOR: Which two blacks?

YOUNG MAN: Those over there.

DOCTOR: (*Looks at the MEN on the bench.*) They're not black.

YOUNG MAN: Not on top, but they are underneath. They're as black as spades underneath, but don't worry about them Doctor, I need medical attention.

DOCTOR: Right, shirt off. What's wrong with you?

YOUNG MAN: I've got bad habits.

DOCTOR: What kind of habits?

YOUNG MAN: I don't know. You see my mother was the only one that knew what they were, and she's dead, but I know they're not physical, there's nothing at all wrong with me physically in a physical sense, I know, because I've always kept myself out of contact with disease, I've even changed my address and kept the new one secret, just to avoid it.

DOCTOR: And you know nothing about these habits?

YOUNG MAN: No ...

DOCTOR: You see no manifestation of them at all?

YOUNG MAN: No Doctor.

DOCTOR: Mmm, most odd. It could mean that you may not have them, you know.

YOUNG MAN: Oh no. I've got them all right Doctor. My mother, if she was alive, would tell you that. She was very worried about them.

DOCTOR: And she wouldn't tell you what they were?

YOUNG MAN: No. She was a very secretive person. My sister won't tell me either, and I'm sure she knows, but we're not speaking, me and her.

DOCTOR: Can't you make it up with her, just till you discover your habits, I mean.

YOUNG MAN: No, it's gone too far. You see, er, would you ask the lady to go?

DOCTOR: Why?

YOUNG MAN: I can't tell you why we fell out, not in front of her.

DOCTOR: But she's a nurse.

YOUNG MAN: She's still a woman, and I'm shy of women. They make me feel nervous.

DOCTOR: Would you go nurse?

The NURSE goes off.

YOUNG MAN: (*Watching her go.*) Well, you see, I, er ...
I keep dreaming you see ...

DOCTOR: We all dream.

YOUNG MAN: But every night, and I keep dreaming I'm
this marvellous looking girl you see, and all these fellows,
they keep chatting me up, they won't leave me alone, they
won't, and one of them, the worst one, well he's my
brother-in-law, and he won't leave me alone, and he's
supposed to love my sister he is, he's supposed to be
married to her. And the way he acts at home too, real
sly he is. You'd think butter wouldn't melt in his mouth.
Churchgoer too. Oh, very sanctimonious he is at home.
And I'm frightened, Doctor, I'm worried in case
I let myself give in to him, and I might fall for a baby
by him, and I don't want to get myself pregnant do I?
Especially with my sister's husband.

DOCTOR: But it's only a dream.

YOUNG MAN: Oh it's no dream. It's real enough at
night. I don't mind telling you. It might seem like a
dream in the day time, but it's no dream at night,
and I think she suspects.

DOCTOR: Who?

YOUNG MAN: My sister, that's why we're not speaking.
I've been wondering whether I ought to tell her.

DOCTOR: About your dream you mean?

YOUNG MAN: Yes. I thought if I told her she'd know
then it wasn't my fault, that it was him to blame.
I mean, she'd see him as he really is.

DOCTOR: Has your brother-in-law ever tried to molest you in the day time?

YOUNG MAN: What, you mean when I'm awake? When I'm not dreaming that I'm a girl?

DOCTOR: Yes.

YOUNG MAN: No ... Oh no. He's too cunning for that. He knows I'd have something on him then properly. I could go to the police about him then. But you can't go to the police about what people do to you in your dreams, can you? And he knows that.

DOCTOR: Hm ... I think the best thing we can do, you know, is to arrange for you to see a psychiatrist.

YOUNG MAN: (*Suspiciously.*) You're not trying to get me certified, are you?

DOCTOR: Certified? No, just see him and explain your problem.

YOUNG MAN: I'm not mad you know.

DOCTOR: No one has said you are.

YOUNG MAN: I'm not bonkers. Just cos my brother-in-law thinks I'm a woman, that don't make me bonkers. He's the one that's a bit touched if you ask me. I'm no whore you know, even if he does think I am. (*He looks round in alarm at the BLIND MAN and the BACKWARDS MAN.*) Don't tell these blacks anything about this, will you? Only if they suspected anything like that ... I mean, you know what they're like. They're very loose morally. They're no idea of chastity.

DOCTOR: They're not blacks.

YOUNG MAN: They look a bit on the white side, I know,

but that's only the weather over here. They're not used to it. Oh God, I'm frightened to go to sleep in case I get raped.

DOCTOR: Look, go and see this chap. He may be able to help. (*He hands the YOUNG MAN a note he has been writing.*) He's a first-class man.

YOUNG MAN: Will he be able to cure my habits?

DOCTOR: I don't know, but he may be able to discover what they are.

YOUNG MAN: That would be a relief, Doctor, it's not knowing that's so terrifying. Thank you. I'll go and see him now. (*He walks off, setting each foot down deliberately, walking on the lines in the paving stones. As he walks:*) Walk on the line, your mother's kind. Walk on the square, your mother don't care. Walk on the line, your mother's kind. Walk on the square, your mother don't care. Walk on the line, your mother's kind, walk on the square, your mother don't care ... (*etc. until he has gone.*)

A GIRL walks on. The DOCTOR approaches her.

DOCTOR: Ah, would you get undressed, please?

GIRL: Get undressed?

DOCTOR: Oh, it's all right, I'm a doctor.

GIRL: But I'm not ill.

DOCTOR: You must allow me to be the judge of that. Now come along, remove your dress. I want to examine you.

GIRL: I don't want to be examined.

DOCTOR: You'll have to. There's a war on you know.

GIRL: War?

DOCTOR: On disease, and if you expect us doctors to cure your diseases we can't afford to sit about in Harley Street waiting for you to bring them to us. We've got to get out and attack them. And to do that we've got to have complete access to your bodies, and be able to examine them wherever we find them. Whether it be on buses, trains, in the streets, the cinema or the theatre. We doctors must have the unassailable right to examine you everywhere and anywhere.

The NURSE returns.

GIRL: I know you have to examine us, but you can't make us take our clothes off anywhere. We've got rights you know.

DOCTOR: So you may have, but there's a war on, and I've got no time to stand here discussing ethics. Your bodies are the battlefield against disease, they must be examined.

GIRL: It's my body, isn't it?

DOCTOR: Oh, yes, but the health and cleanliness of it is everybody's concern, and as a Medical Health Officer I demand Society's right to inspect it. Dress off.

GIRL: I'll write to my MP about this.

DOCTOR: As you wish. But this is a democracy don't forget, and I have MP's as well as you have. Get the vaccines ready, nurse, but a screen for the young lady. There's no need for her to be embarrassed more than necessary. (*To the GIRL.*) Now, let's have a look at you. (*He listens on the stethoscope.*) Hm, I don't like the sound of that chest. Open your mouth. (*He tuts.*) Tut, tut, tut ...

(*To the NURSE.*) She's still got tonsils in there. We'll have to get those out, nurse.

GIRL: Why?

DOCTOR: Because they're the main cause of tonsilitis, that's why. I suppose you've still got your appendix too, have you?

GIRL: No. I have had that out.

DOCTOR: Well that's something. Hmm. Do these legs give you any trouble?

GIRL: No, Doctor.

DOCTOR: Nevertheless I should have them off if I were you.

GIRL: Have them off? What, my legs? Eh? What are you talking about?

DOCTOR: Well, they're not much use to you that I can see of them. What's your occupation?

GIRL: Manicurist.

DOCTOR: You don't manicure with your legs, do you?

GIRL: No, but I have to walk about on them though.

DOCTOR: You can walk about on artificial legs. The way they're making them now they are much better than the natural ones, which admits that we are heading towards a more legless society, what with motor cars, and television.

GIRL: But I want my own legs.

DOCTOR: Very well. I haven't the power to remove them without your consent, but an operation to remove them would be safest.

GIRL: Safest. But there's nothing wrong with them.

DOCTOR: No, but you could soon get something wrong with them. You've only got to knock them, or damage them in any way. If I told you the amount of leg diseases there are, you'd be horrified, and having natural legs such as these makes you vulnerable to all of them. They're like tonsils, appendix, teeth, useless appendages, cut down on the useless parts of our bodies and it leaves the germs a smaller area to breed in.

GIRL: Well, why don't you have your legs off, then?

DOCTOR: I've had them off. In my job, facing disease all day long, every precaution has to be taken.

GIRL: Well, I'm not having mine off.

DOCTOR: All right I can't force you. (*He turns to the NURSE.*) You see nurse, this is the worst battle we have to fight, the ignorance of the unscientific mind. The damage done by sceptics and their bloody doubts: The omniscience of the medical profession is being destroyed. The blind faith we were once able to instil has given place to fear and disbelief. What's the point of being a specialist if you've got to explain to the man in the street what you're doing?

NURSE: Never mind, sir. We'll win through in the end. The public are always slow to accept new ideas.

GIRL: New ideas! What ... eh ... having my legs off!

DOCTOR: But my dear girl. I can replace those primitive old-fashioned legs of yours with brand new mechanical ones. Disease-free legs. Legs that can walk for miles without tiring. Legs you don't have to put up after a hard day, or buy shoes for. Modern, mechanical, labour-saving legs that can't go wrong or wear out.

But you'd sooner walk around on those silly old legs.
I mean, good heavens, look at them.

GIRL: You're not taking them off, anyway.

DOCTOR: Why not?

GIRL: But ... what's a girl without legs?

DOCTOR: (*Studies her legs.*) You think science and art together can't do better than that? (*To the NURSE.*) Show her those new Dior legs, and the Balmains.

The NURSE lifts her skirts high to reveal her own legs.

NURSE: Look at mine, these are by Yves Saint Laurent.

DOCTOR: (*To the GIRL.*) You see, and they're finished in permanent suntan.

NURSE: And you can get them in gold and silver lame finish for evening wear, with the super flesh touch.

GIRL: (*Excited.*) They're marvellous. (*Admiring them.*) Really fab they are ...

DOCTOR: And they never grow old, warp or get knobbly.

NURSE: And no ugly hairs, spots or blemishes to worry about.

GIRL: That's great. They're really fab. (*Excitedly.*) Oh Doctor, when can you remove these and fit me with legs like that?

DOCTOR: Immediately. And you can have them under the National Health too.

GIRL: What nothing to pay?

DOCTOR: Nothing at all. It comes under the State Plan of Health. For narrowing the areas of disease in the body. Prepare the patient for the operation.

The NURSE leads the GIRL away. As the DOCTOR follows
them the UNDERTAKER and SEXTON appear from
behind the tombstone. The UNDERTAKER watches the
DOCTOR with a scowl.

UNDERTAKER: I don't like him working here.

SEXTON: What him?

UNDERTAKER: The cleverer he gets, the more he slows
things down here. It used to be pretty brisk here in the
old days. I've seen the figures in the old books, very
busy it was. They were in here before they were
twenty, most of 'em, until people like Pasteur and
Jenner came along with their bloody cure-alls, or
nearly cure-alls, keeping 'em alive till they're past
seventy now they are. And them socialists as well,
they haven't helped, improving conditions like they
have. They're all frightened to die, that's their trouble,
all frightened they are. I mean, to hear 'em talk you
wouldn't think there was any heaven or after life, would
you? I mean, the way they're all hanging on down here.
The aristocracy's the best. They're the only ones who
don't seem to bother. As soon as they're born they have
their tomb made. Well, I mean, at least there's planning
there. It shows a bit of planning. Still never mind.
Things are brightening up a bit now. I mean, this bomb
they've got that's going to do a lot of good, I reckon, as
soon as they drop it. But there again, you see, I mean,
they won't plan it. They'll just drop it without any
warning. I mean, if they was logical, they could come
to me, to the trade like, and say, Right we're dropping
the bomb on the seventeenth of March, 1969, Tuesday
afternoon, three o'clock. All I'd have to do then is to
get that in writing, go to the bank and they'd advance
me the money so I could corner all the land, and get
the boxes made.

SEXTON: Get a big fire going.

UNDERTAKER: Of course, but keep the brass handles, don't burn them.

SEXTON: I mean, you don't want to start digging that lot down. You don't want to have to dig for all that crowd.

UNDERTAKER: But they won't do it. They won't plan anything. That's the trouble. There's absolutely no planning done at all these days.

He wanders off. The SEXTON looks after him.

SEXTON: Him and his blooming aristocracy. No, they ain't frightened to die. No, of course they ain't. Cos it's made for them up there. They've got it laid on. (*He turns to the camera.*) Isn't it marvellous, eh? It's not even our bleedin' world. It's not even our bleedin' heaven.

~

PART TWO

The VICAR comes on carrying a bill poster, bucket of paste and some posters. He proceeds to stick a poster on the vault. It reads, 'Keep Heaven White'. The SEXTON wanders over and reads it.

SEXTON: Hm ... (*He nods in agreement.*) Hm ... they're getting 'em barred up there too, are they?

VICAR: (*Indicating the poster.*) That's got nothing to do with the colour bar.

SEXTON: Oh ... I thought ...

VICAR: Not physically. Not on the physical side. A man's skin is his own affair. Black, yellow, brown or white ... he's entitled to be what he is, and I respect that right. It's purely his own business. But the soul – is something different. Ah yes. There I'm afraid, his rights vanish. His privileges of self-ownership don't exist. The soul can be only one colour. God's colour. White. Pure white. Yes, that's where we must have discrimination. That's where we need the colour bar, that's where we need the prejudice. Keep heaven white. Reserved and strictly private for those with white souls.

SEXTON: You mean ... no blacks'll get in up there?

VICAR: No. Black is the colour of sin in the varying shades of grievousness. And one tiny black stain of sin on any soul will bar it from heaven and the Lord's presence. On this, God must be dogmatic, farseeing and unforgiving. And he must see that none wheedle their way in with these damn death bed conversions. They make a mock of holiness. They must be stopped. God must disallow them. They indulge every sin the flesh is capable of ... and then, when they're about to die ...

when there is no more chance of recovery ... they call in a priest and ask for absolution and get their souls re-whitened. It's got to stop. It's not fair. God in his wisdom has got to realise that you can't liberalise on sin. He's got to ban these re-whites and keep heaven pure white.

He picks up his pot of paste and posters and moves off. The old SEXTON stands still looking at the poster. The YOUNG MAN returns.

YOUNG MAN: Excuse me, I'm looking for a psychiatrist ... you don't know where I'll find one do you?

SEXTON: I dunno ... which one you looking for?

YOUNG MAN: Oh, I don't know. Anyone would do I should think. They're all about the same I suppose. Some better than others – but that's all. I've got a letter for him, you see.

SEXTON: 'nt it got an address on it, then?

YOUNG MAN: Yes, but I can't find it.

SEXTON: What is it? What is the address?

YOUNG MAN: Oh no. I'm sorry. I can't do that. This address was given to me in strict confidence. I can't give that away. If I disclose that ... he'd have hundreds of nutcases banging on his door ... Hello ... (*He looks at the poster.*) Who put that up?

SEXTON: The vicar.

YOUNG MAN: Excellent. Action from the church at last, eh? Very good. Keep heaven white. Excellent idea. The GPO should do something like this too. Segregated pillar boxes ... that's what we need. That could cut down on postal diseases. We're entitled to them. We're entitled to some protection from the GPO I mean, the way it is now ... you could post a letter and it could be left lying beside some black one all night long ...

SEXTON: What letter you mean?

YOUNG MAN: Not only your letters, but your daughter's letters too ... and how would you like that eh? How would you like one of your daughter's letters ... perhaps a love letter ... left lying alongside some black one ... all night, eh?

SEXTON: I ain't got a daughter. But I don't hold in with mixed marriages though.

YOUNG MAN: Nor mixed pillar boxes. Why should you? Why should you have to? This is a free country and if you want segregation, you're entitled to have segregation. (*He looks at the poster again.*) Yes, I agree with that. Keep heaven white ... good old vicar ... (*To the SEXTON.*) Don't you agree with it?

SEXTON: Well not really, I mean ... you see ... I don't go on all that religion see. What I reckon ... I reckon that God this God ... is too upper-class. That's his trouble ... that's what's wrong with him, mate.

YOUNG MAN: Too upper-class?

SEXTON: Yer ... that's his trouble ... and what I reckon ... I reckon the working class ought to get its own working-class God, with a sort of working-class heaven.

YOUNG MAN: A working-class God? But ... no ... I mean, wait a minute. You can't treat God like that ... I mean, you can't go around having all different Gods for all different classes. You can't have more than one God. There's only one God you know.

SEXTON: Yer ... I know ... that's what I'm saying ... but what I'm saying ... see ... is there ought to be two ...

I mean, take them blacks ... them coloureds ... I mean, they're got their own God ain't they?

YOUNG MAN: The blacks ...

SEXTON: Yer ... they've got their own black God ... they have. That Mohammed ... you know. Buddha. He looks after them. But the working-class see ... they ain't got no one ... I mean, when we die ... us working-class ... I mean, the only heaven we got is this tory heaven ... this Eton and Harrow one. This Lord God's place. I mean, there you are, 'nt it ... Lord God ... Lord God ... see ... not Fred God or Harry God ... Oh no ... a titled God ... a Lord God. A stuck-up, toffee-nosed God ... a guvnors God ... I mean, look at his bishops, look at that lot ... they're all nobs ... they're all out of big houses ... living in palaces they are. No, what I say ... what I say we need ... is some working-class bishops ... some council house bishops.

YOUNG MAN: But you've got to have guvnors ... I mean, you've got to have people in charge running things, you can't do without that ... you can't do without guvnors.

SEXTON: I ain't saying you can ... I'm not saying you can do without 'em ... not down here ... but up there ... I mean, it ought to be different ... up there ... didn't it? I mean it's supposed to be eternal peace 'nt it? Rest in peace ... but I don't see how you're going to get any rest in ... with a load of guvnors chasing you about.

YOUNG MAN: There's not much of the Christian in you is there eh? You ain't got much of the bloody Christian in you, have you?

SEXTON: Eh? I'm Christian ... I'm as Christian as anyone else.

YOUNG MAN: You believe in Christ? You mean to say you believe in Christ?

SEXTON: Yer ...

The BLIND MAN has got up and, followed by the BACKWARDS MAN, still walking backwards, taps his way over to the SEXTON and YOUNG MAN.

YOUNG MAN: Then why are you attacking his father like that? Eh? Why are you having a go at his dad?

BLIND MAN: You back again, Sambo?

YOUNG MAN: Look, don't you call me that. I'm no black and you know it.

BLIND MAN: You're not white, Sambo. I told you before, you're black ... as black as a pot.

YOUNG MAN: I'm not black, I'm white.

BLIND MAN: Well, I prefer to think of you as black, shiny, coal black.

YOUNG MAN: (*Very agitated.*) But you've no right to ... You've got no right to think of me as black. I'm white. I really am. Tell him. Tell him I'm white.

SEXTON: Well, you are ain't you? I mean, he is white. I mean, as far as I can see, he is ... I mean, he's not black.

BLIND MAN: I say he is. To me he's black, To me he is just a black-faced coon, that's all he is to me.

YOUNG MAN: (*Almost in tears.*) But I'm not ... I'm not black. (*To the BACKWARDS MAN.*) You're his friend ... can't you tell him I'm white?

BACKWARDS MAN: How am I to know what colour you are? I can't see you any more than he can.

YOUNG MAN: But you're not blind ... open your eyes ... open your eyes and look at me ... and tell him I'm white.

BACKWARDS MAN: It wouldn't do any good. He's a freethinker. He thinks exactly what he wants to think. If he thinks you're black then to him you're black ... and that's all there is to it.

YOUNG MAN: But that's not all there is to it ... I don't want him thinking I'm black.

SEXTON: I wouldn't worry about it if I were you. I mean, what does it matter what he thinks ...?

YOUNG MAN: It might not matter to you what he thinks because he isn't thinking anything about you. But it matters to me. I don't want people going around thinking I'm black. How would you like it if he went around thinking you were black?

SEXTON: Yer ... I can see your point mate ... but I mean ... just 'cos he thinks you're black ... I mean, it don't make you black ... does it? I mean, you see my meaning?

YOUNG MAN: Look, it does to him. It makes me black to him.

SEXTON: Oh yer ... I suppose it does ... but ... I mean, only to him.

YOUNG MAN: But I don't want to be black to anyone. If he goes around thinking I'm black ... I mean, black I become, don't I? I become black to him. In his thoughts I'm black.

BLIND MAN: Coal black.

YOUNG MAN: Well, I'm not going to have it. I'm not going to have him seeing me like that. I mean, you let him get away with that, and the next thing he'll do will be dreaming about me ... and then I'll be black in his dreams too ... and being placed in positions ... I mean, positions that I'm not entitled to be placed in. Humiliating positions. Positions with no rights or privileges ... and who is he to make me black and deprive me of my privileges ...? And another thing, he won't only be dreaming about me will he? Oh no. There'll be other people in his dreams ... all sorts of people ... and they'll see me as black ... I mean, that sort of thing could spread. I know. I know what dreams are like. I have them myself.

SEXTON: We all have dreams ...

YOUNG MAN: But not dreams like I do ...

BLIND MAN: All right, Sambo. That's enough. We've heard enough. Stow it now and get back to your own side of town.

YOUNG MAN: You leave me alone. I've as much right to be here as anyone.

BLIND MAN: Oh, getting Bolshie, eh Sambo? Getting a bit full of yourself are you? Well, we'll have to see what a good hard clout over that black curly nut will do for putting those kind of ideas out of it.

YOUNG MAN: You leave me alone ...

BLIND MAN: Oh, you want to be left alone now, do you? Isn't it marvellous? The bloody rights these people want. Show them a bit of kindness and the next thing ... they're demanding it.

The YOUNG MAN moves away as the BLIND MAN jabs about with his stick, trying to find him.

YOUNG MAN: Leave me alone ... don't touch me. You're the black ... you're the one that's black.

BLIND MAN: Oh no, Sambo ... you can't pull that one again. It won't work this time. There's no more doubts in my mind as to who's black and who's white. You're the black all right.

YOUNG MAN: So are you ... so are you black.

BLIND MAN: Isn't it marvellous, eh? If he can't be white like me he wants me to be black like him, Bloody equality mad they are ... these underdogs. They just won't face up to what they are and take their medicine ... Come on, where are you ... you're due for a beating ... it's time you were beaten.

YOUNG MAN: You leave me alone.

We hear the sound of bugle and drum and the OFFICER and PRIVATE march on. The YOUNG MAN runs over to them.

Help ... help ... help me please.

OFFICER: (*Stops blowing his bugle.*) Halt!

The PRIVATE halts. To the YOUNG MAN.

What's the matter.

YOUNG MAN: It's him ... the blind man ... he's trying to turn me into a black.

OFFICER: Trying to turn you into a black?

BLIND MAN: Who's that? Who is it? Who are they?

BACKWARDS MAN: It sounds like the military ...

SEXTON: It's the army ...

BLIND MAN: What do they want?

BACKWARDS MAN: They want to know what's going on.

BLIND MAN: Just like the police, eh? Bloody nosey ...

He taps his way over to the OFFICER and runs his hand guidingly over him. He finds his shoulder and feels the pips.

Officer, eh? Captain.

He then runs his hand along the OFFICER's outstretched arm, the one holding the gun. He touches the gun and then the PRIVATE's face and head, and then the gun again.

And holding a gun at someone's head too. (*He taps away and then turns back.*) Why are you holding a gun to his head?

OFFICER: I have to. It's the only way to keep him in uniform.

BLIND MAN: I see. Hm. That's what young Sambo here needs ... a gun at his head. Put a gun to his head and he'd behave more like a black to me.

OFFICER: But ... I don't understand. Why do you want to make him into a black?

BLIND MAN: (*Indicating the PRIVATE.*) Why do you want to make him into a soldier ...?

OFFICER: I need a soldier. I'm an officer. An army officer. And it's no good being an officer in the army without a soldier is it?

BLIND MAN: Well, I need a black. I'm white you see. Pure white. And there's no joy in being white if there's no black, is there?

OFFICER: Yes, I see that. But he isn't black. You're just inventing him. You're trying to make him black ... trying to turn him into a black.

BLIND MAN: (*Jabs his stick into the PRIVATE.*) And you're inventing him. He's not a real soldier. You don't have to hold a gun at a real soldier's head to make him wear a uniform. A real soldier is proud to wear the uniform. You're just trying to make him into a soldier.

OFFICER: And you're trying to make him into a black.

BLIND MAN: That's right.

OFFICER: But he doesn't want to be a black.

BLIND MAN: (*Jabbing the PRIVATE.*) And he doesn't want to be a black. But you need your soldier. And I need my black. You've got your black ... and I want my black.

OFFICER: Black? What black? I've got no black.

BLIND MAN: (*Jabbing the PRIVATE.*) Him. He's your black. Your soldier black.

OFFICER: Eh? What are you talking about man? You're a black man. (*He indicates the PRIVATE.*) He's not black. He's white. (*He indicates the YOUNG MAN.*) As white as this young fellow here.

BLIND MAN: All right. So he's white ... a white black. They're both white blacks. Who cares what colour they are ... so long as they're blacks. I told you, I'm blind. I don't deal in colours.

OFFICER: You're mad.

YOUNG MAN: (*From behind the OFFICER.*) He's mad all right. He's off his nut. He wants putting away ... that's what he wants. He's the one that wants to see the psychiatrist.

BLIND MAN: Look, he might have a white skin ... this soldier boy here ... (*He jabs him again.*) But that don't prove he's not a black. Not to me, it doesn't. He's segregated isn't he? He's not allowed to mix. You've

segregated him. You know you have. You've trained
him to feel inferior to you.

OFFICER: Yes ... but good heavens man, he's in the army.
He's a soldier. He's got to have superior officers.

BLIND MAN: Very well then. I'm not saying he hasn't.
But if you want your inferiors in the army, we want our
inferiors in civvy street. We're all the same you know.
We're only human.

SEXTON: He's got you there, 'nt he? I can see that. It's
human nature that is. It's like me ... I been segregated,
I been segregated all my life I have ... segregated into
the slums, I was ... just because of me parents that's all.
No other reason. That was the reason for it.

BLIND MAN: What colour were your parents ?

SEXTON: What, my mum and dad ... Oh ... Well, they
must have been that colour ... you was saying ... you
know ... them white blacks. Yer, that's what colour they
was. They was all that colour down where we lived ...
must have been blacks I suppose ... that turned white ...
that's what they must have been ... 'cos, I mean they
wasn't allowed to mix with the others ... you know,
them real whites ... them white whites ... It's like them
black blacks.

OFFICER: Black blacks? What black blacks?

SEXTON: Them black ones. The proper ones. The black
blacks. Like them white whites ... that's what they're
like ... Well, they live like 'em don't they? They live the
same ... they don't live like the other blacks ... if you
see what I mean. I seen some ... They had 'em up at the
palace ... invited to tea, they was ... all dressed up in
silk they was, and covered in diamonds. Indian Blacks
some of 'em ... most of 'em ... but real blacks ... you
know ... black blacks.

YOUNG MAN: Well I don't want to be any kind of black. I don't. Black black or white black. I came from a good home I did ... I'm no old rubbish ... (*He indicates the SEXTON.*) I'm not like him ... I'm not supposed to be segregated. (*He indicates the BLIND MAN.*) Not by him or anyone else ... I can segregate myself I can ... If I want to be segregated ... I'm one of the segregators, I am. I was brought up to it, I went to a good school I did. No elementary rubbish. (*To the BLIND MAN.*) Look, you might not be able to see colours but you can hear sounds ... you can tell tones, and there's no black in my voice. My mother and father paid a lot for this voice ... and they were very fussy, they were. They were very fussy about voices. About the colour of voices.

BLIND MAN: Listen to it. An educated black. A well-schooled coon.

SEXTON: He sounds like a bit of a guvnor to me, he does ... he's got a touch of guvnor he has. He's got more of the guvnor than the black in him.

BLIND MAN: Yes, well, we can soon knock that out of him. We can soon get rid of that.

OFFICER: You know, you're right. The only way this problem can be solved is to put a gun at his head. If he turns black ... it's his right colour.

YOUNG MAN: (*Laughs.*) No, no ... please ... please ... don't ... don't make me black.

BLIND MAN: (*Laughs.*) He's a black all right.

BACKWARDS MAN: He's turning black fast.

OFFICER: Yes. (*He puts his gun at the YOUNG MAN's head.*) Down, dog ... down. On your knees. (*The YOUNG MAN kneels down.*) That's better. I'll get my chap to black him up for you now.

BLIND MAN: Your soldier ... he won't turn without the gun at his head?

OFFICER: No. He's quite safe. He's had a gun at his head so long now, he won't even notice it's been taken away. (*To the PRIVATE.*) Attention! Blacking at the ready. (*They do it as a kind of drill.*) Blacking ... begin ... (*To the BLIND MAN.*) These blacks are very good at blacking each other.

The PRIVATE proceeds to black the YOUNG MAN's face. He doesn't resist, just kneels trembling. When the PRIVATE is finished he stands back at attention again and the OFFICER inspects his work.

OFFICER: A real white black. Come on sing us some of those white black songs. (*He sings himself.*) Mammy, mammy ... Come on. (*He sings again.*) Sit upon my knee sonny boy, though you're only three, sonny boy ...

BLIND MAN: Tote that bale, tote that bale.

OFFICER: (*Jabbing the gun into the YOUNG MAN's head.*) Come on man, give out with some of that old white black talk. Yes sir, massa ... Uncle Tom ... Cobblers an all ...

The UNDERTAKER walks on, stops and watches.

UNDERTAKER: Hello, what have we got here, then ...?

BLIND MAN: It's a white black minstrel show ...

OFFICER: He wants to be white. It's a black who wants to be white.

UNDERTAKER: Does he ... I bet he does. Still, I don't mind them so much ... the blacks ... it's the others. It's the others ... the white foreigners ... they're the ones I hate. At least the blacks are honest. You can tell them

right away. You can see what they are by their skin ...
But the others ... the bloody French and Germans. You
can fraternise with them without knowing ... you find
yourself mixing with them. Even liking them. That's
the terrible thing ... even liking them.

*The DOCTOR walks on. The YOUNG MAN gets up and
runs towards him.*

YOUNG MAN: Doctor, Doctor ... They've turned me into
a black ... look. They've made me black.

DOCTOR: Don't worry about it. It's only a pigmentation
of the skin.

YOUNG MAN: It's not ... it's not. It's more than that ...
I know it is. I used to be a Jew, so I know. Have you
ever been a Jew? No ... I don't suppose you have ...
You're one of the lucky ones. You've never been
anything unpleasant. Well I have. I've been one ...
all of my family was ... and it's bloody rotten ... it is ...
it's almost as bad as being black.

A WOMAN walks on ... a large JEWISH WOMAN.

WOMAN: Oh. Excuse me ... I hope I'm not interrupting
anything, only I'm looking for someone. A boy ...
a young man. He's my son. He hasn't been home for
several days, and I'm rather worried about him. You
see he's not ... he's not quite right in the head. He's
inclined to be fanciful, imagining ... you know.
Imagines he's what he ain't like. He upsets me. And
I worry. He keeps telling people I'm dead ... I'm sure
he don't mean no harm by it ... but it's upsetting.

YOUNG MAN: Mum.

WOMAN: (*Looking at him.*) Morrie ... what have you done ..?

YOUNG MAN: I've turned black ... they've turned me
black ... they've made me into a black.

WOMAN: I knew something like this would happen. I kept telling you, but you wouldn't listen. You would go your own way.

YOUNG MAN: Take me home mum ...

WOMAN: What, like that? What do you think your father would say? Oh no. You wouldn't be a Jew like us ... oh no. But you'll be a black. Oh yes, you don't mind being a black. Well, you've made your own bed ... now you can lay on it 'cos I'm not having no blacks in my house.

She turns and strides off in high dudgeon.

YOUNG MAN: Mum ... mum it's not my fault. I didn't do it. It wasn't me.

BLIND MAN: So ... you used to be a Jew, did you?

YOUNG MAN: It's none of your business what I used to be.

BLIND MAN: Don't get lippy now, Sambo ... watch the old lip there. We're entitled to know what you are. We don't want your sort round here lowering our land values ... (*He walks over to the YOUNG MAN and feels his nose.*) Yes, he's Jewish all right ... I've tweaked enough of their noses to know that.

OFFICER: He hasn't got a Jewish nose. He doesn't look a bit Jewish.

BLIND MAN: You don't want to let his looks take you in. That's the trouble with you people who can see ... you let 'em fool you with their looks.

BACKWARDS MAN: He's probably had plastic surgery anyway.

BLIND MAN: Course he has. They ought to be put down those bloody plastic surgeons. For a few bob they'd make any Jew a Christian they would. They'll be starting on the blacks soon, giving them white skins. And then where will we be? Right up the creek, if you ask me.

BACKWARDS MAN: With no one left to hate but ourselves.

BLIND MAN: We must have something to hate apart from ourselves. Something to blame our failure on to.

The VICAR and PRIEST enter.

DOCTOR: But Judaism is only a religion, and colour just a pigmentation of the skin.

BLIND MAN: Oh, don't listen to him ... he's got excuses for everything. Jew ... a religion ... colour ... a pigmentation. If God had wanted the blacks to be white, he would have made 'em white in the first place. He was no fool.

DOCTOR: How do you know what colour God is? God might be black for all you know.

YOUNG MAN: And a Jew.

BLIND MAN: Blasphemers ... I'll knock you both down, you talk like that about God. God is white ... He's beautiful and white and he lives in a beautiful white house ... in a beautiful white heaven ... surrounded by well-trimmed English lawns.

BACKWARDS MAN: He wears a bowler hat and striped pants ... and carried a furled umbrella.

SEXTON: He's upper-class ... a snob and a toff ...

BLIND MAN: And he hates Jews and blacks ... especially black Jews like Sambo here.

PRIEST: God is love ... he doesn't hate.

VICAR: All God hates is sin.

BLIND MAN: And sin is black. You know the colour of
sin, Father. It's black ... ugly black.

VICAR: Yes, but it's sin not skins that God is interested in.

PRIEST: Definitely sins, skins he's not interested in.

YOUNG MAN: The son of God was a Jew.

BLIND MAN: Lies ... Jewish lies ... God would never have
let his son be a Jew. God was English ... and an English
gentleman ... like his Bishops.

PRIEST: God made everyone.

VICAR: Everyone.

BLIND MAN: Except the Jews and the blacks.

YOUNG MAN: Who made them, then?

VICAR: God made them ... in his own image.

PRIEST: Definitely everyone in his own image.

BLIND MAN: No ... it's lies ... you're telling lies. You
aren't fit to wear the cloth when you talk like that.
If God made him, that black Sambo there, then send
him back to God. Put a rejection slip on him ... doesn't
conform to Christian standard.

BACKWARDS MAN: Hear, hear, and if God is black ...
reject God.

BLIND MAN: God isn't black. You've only got to see his
picture to know that.

DOCTOR: Have you seen his pictures?

BLIND MAN: I've had them described to me ... and
they sound wonderful. Great works of art and in them,

God ... is white and beautiful, and he made us white and beautiful in his own image.

BACKWARDS MAN: God is on our side. He's one of us.

SEXTON: He's not on my side ... he's a capitalist ... that's what God is ... the biggest property owner on earth. That's what he is.

BLIND MAN: Enough talk ... let's put this black down. Let's do ourselves a favour and get rid of him.

OFFICER: Kill him?

BLIND MAN: Yes ... Why not? It'll give your soldier boy some practice. He's got to be trained to kill ... and the more experience he gets at it, the better he'll be when the time comes. And come it will. It'll help the Doctor too. He's a liberal and if we get rid of the black it puts an end to the colour bar.

BACKWARDS MAN: True ... without Jews or blacks there can be no race hatreds.

BLIND MAN: Don't worry about that. We'll cross that bridge when we come to it.

SEXTON: It'll provide a bit of work for my guvnor. He doesn't care how he gets his corpses ... as long as he gets 'em.

VICAR and PRIEST: What about us?

BLIND MAN: You'll do better out of it than most of us. It'll provide you with a great sin ... a crime against humanity. You trade in sins, Vicar, sin is indispensable to you. It's indispensable to any society organised by vicars. You live on sin, and when we repent ... we submit to you. We can't go to God personally and repent. We have to come to you.

DOCTOR: And what about him?

(*He indicates the YOUNG MAN.*)

The young man you're going to kill.

BLIND MAN: He'll do well too. It'll provide both his races with a martyr.

YOUNG MAN: No ... no ... I don't want to die ...

DOCTOR: (*Kindly.*) Don't worry son ... we all have to go some day. How and when is not very important really. When you've gone ... you'll be regarded much higher by these people. When Hitler killed his millions of Jews, he struck a great blow against anti-semitism ... and throughout Europe the Jew rose to a crest of popularity he had never achieved before. The Jew was the humanity that Hitler's crime was against ... and every man was on their side.

VICAR: But Doctor, you're not going to stand by and let these people murder this boy, are you?

DOCTOR: It's for the good of his race. They'll never achieve their freedom from oppression except through violence. Someone must die to save them. Every race must have its martyr. If it's not him, it'll be someone else ... and it's not for us to choose. We who can't distinguish one Negro from another.

YOUNG MAN: I'm not a Negro.

DOCTOR: Your face is black ... you must play your part.

YOUNG MAN: It's boot polish ... they're blacked my face with boot polish.

DOCTOR: What is the difference between pigmentation and boot polish? They've chosen you to play the coon.

You've got to let them kill you tonight so that we who are decent can revile their crime against you.

(*A JUDGE in full robes appears accompanied by the UNDERTAKER.*)

JUDGE: Come along ... get on with your murder ... I've waited long enough.

PRIEST: You support this crime, Judge?

JUDGE: I support all crime ... without crime I couldn't exist. I'm no different to you, and him, Father. You thrive on sin, I thrive on crime ... as the Doctor here thrives on disease and the soldier thrives on war.

UNDERTAKER: As I thrive on death.

DOCTOR: As the decent liberals among us thrive on injustice.

BLIND MAN: And I thrive on hate.

BACKWARDS MAN: We must all kill him, so that we may all continue to thrive.

OFFICER: (*To the YOUNG MAN.*) Do you want a blindfold?

YOUNG MAN: No ... I want to see who fires the gun.

DOCTOR: We shall all fire the gun. The soldier will merely point it.

OFFICER: Fire!

There is a report and the YOUNG MAN falls back into the open grave.

DOCTOR: Well that's that.

JUDGE: Yes ... now the trial can begin.

PRIEST: And repentance for the sin ...

He starts to murmur the confessional.

They all kneel down.

ALL: Pray Father forgive us for we have sinned ... It's no time at all since our last confession but we accuse ourselves of ... we have killed a man because of the colour of his skin ... for these and all our other sins which we cannot now remember, we humbly ask penance from you and pardon from God ...

Fade on the PRIEST murmuring the confessional: 'May Our Lord Jesus Christ absolve you etc. etc.'

THE COMPARTMENT

The Compartment was first presented by the BBC in August 1961 with the following cast:

YOUNG MAN, Michael Caine

MAN, Frank Finlay

Directed by John McGrath

1. INT. RAILWAY CARRIAGE. STUDIO. DAY.

A middle-aged MAN sits in a corner seat reading The Times. *He is a very prosperous looking man. He could be a barrister, or a judge, or surgeon or perhaps an MP, maybe even a cabinet minister.*

The carriage door opens and a youngish man gets in carrying a small suitcase. He goes to sit in the corner seat opposite the MAN.

YOUNG MAN: Er ... excuse me ... (*The MAN looks up.*) Er do you mind if I put my case up here?

He indicates the rack above his seat. It is completely empty. The rack on the other side is quite empty too except for a briefcase that belongs to the MAN.

MAN: (*Looks at him rather surprised.*) No ... of course not ...

He goes back to his paper.

YOUNG MAN: It should be all right putting it up here. This part of the rack is reserved for anyone who sits here ... Well not exactly reserved I suppose ... But meant for ... It's meant for the person who sits here ... I should think it's meant for ... But if someone already had their case up here ... I suppose you'd have no grounds for asking them to take it down ... They could refuse I suppose couldn't they ... if their case was up there first – I mean they could refuse ... Well it wouldn't matter ... it's only a small case I could carry it on my knee if it came to that ... or put it on the seat ... I could put it on the seat ... There's plenty of room on the seat ... Yes perhaps I'd better put it on the seat.

He takes it down and puts it on the seat beside him.

It's not in your way there is it ...?

The MAN doesn't answer.

This case ... It's not in your way there is it ...

MAN: (*A trifle uncomfortable.*) Er no ... it's not in my way ...

YOUNG MAN: You're sure? Only it'd be no trouble to move it if it is ... I could put it up on the rack if it's in your way ...

He looks up at the rack.

There's plenty of room up there ... Yes perhaps I'd better put it on the rack ... It'll be out of your way up there.

MAN: Really it's not in my way ... I assure you.

YOUNG MAN: I don't want to be trouble to anyone ... If you'd rather I put it up on the rack ... I don't mind ... It's no trouble to shift it ... It's quite light ... (*Picks it up.*) You see ... it's quite light ... It's only a small case and there's not much in it ... It's empty actually ... Well I'm not going away for long. I'm only staying overnight ... That's why I didn't bother to put anything in it ... I suppose I needn't have brought it really ... But they don't like letting you in hotels if you haven't got a case do they ... That's what I heard. A chap I used to work with told me that ... He said they're not very keen to let you in hotels if you haven't got a case ... Do you think that's true ... Still I suppose it must be true or he wouldn't have told me would he ... Some people do tell lies though ... It's funny isn't it the way some people tell lies. I suppose it's a kink in their character. You're sure it's not in your way there ....

MAN: It's quite all right.

YOUNG MAN: Oh good, only I don't want to be a trouble ... You get so many people these days who are a trouble ... especially on trains ... (*Pause.*) You will tell me if it's in your way there won't you ... (*Pause.*) I think I'll put it on the rack ... It'll be out of your way there ... Anyway this rack is for cases isn't it ...

He puts the case up on the rack. He is about to sit down but stops to read a sign. It is to do with the communication cord.

That's interesting isn't it ... Apparently if you pull this cord they fine you five pounds ... It's not a cord actually it's a chain. No that's not true really ... not about the chain I don't mean ... about pulling it ... It's only for improper use you get fined five pounds ... I wonder what improper use constitutes ... Use of improperly ... not for the use designated ... not proper ... not suitable ... unfit ... unbecoming ... incorrect ... improper fraction ... a fraction whose numerator is greater than its denominator. You see I know all the terms ... I used to read the dictionary quite a lot once ... I suppose if I was to pull it now ... give it a sudden jerk ... that would constitute use not designated ... unbecoming ... use of improperly ... and it would be five pounds up my shirt wouldn't it ...

The MAN is looking at him now in some alarm.

Oh don't worry, I'm not going to pull it ... I couldn't afford the five pounds ... And for proper use ... there's no fine attached to proper use ... There wouldn't be would there ... no point in having it there otherwise ... Now what would constitute proper use .. the use for which it is designated ...
I suppose if you was to suddenly attack me ... that would be the proper use ... I could pull it then ...

The MAN is looking very apprehensively at him.

Or even if you didn't attack me ... I could pull it and
say you did ... especially if I tore some of my clothing ...
and banged my head against the window to make my
nose bleed ... You'd have a job explaining that wouldn't
you ... What would you say to them when they came ...
If I said you made my nose bleed and tore all my
clothes and kept punching me ... You'd had a job
explaining that wouldn't you ...

The MAN looks very alarmed.

Oh don't worry I wouldn't do it ... But it could be done
couldn't it ... I suppose the person would have to be mad
though wouldn't they to do a thing like that ... absolutely
potty I should think ... Still I suppose you could get mad
people on trains ... You don't know who you're riding with
do you ... It's all this nationalisation. The railways have
never been the same since they were nationalised. I don't
think so anyway. Do you? Do you think they've been the
same ... That's why I wouldn't vote for them last time ...
Those Labour people ... I wouldn't vote for them last time
... Well they've fallen down on all their promises haven't
they. So have the others I wouldn't vote for them either ...
I've got an aunt ... She was entitled to thirty shillings ...
and they did her out of it. Winston Churchill it was ...
during the war ... she was entitled to this thirty shillings
you see ... and he wouldn't let her have it. She wrote to the
papers about it but they wouldn't print it. Well they're all
in it together aren't they. Someone had it though, someone
is thirty shillings better off ... Well it stands to reason
doesn't it ... There's thirty shillings floating about in the
government ... superfluous ... a superfluous thirty shillings
... Someone's put it in their pocket obviously ... That's how
they get their big houses ... (*Pause.*) That case is not in
your way is it ...? Only I can easily move it ... It's no
trouble ... (*Pause.*) Yes, that's how they get their big houses
all right ... Have you got a big house ... I should think you

have to look at you ... To look at you I would say you had
a big house ... with grounds ... all laid out in borders ...
I like borders ... I bet you've got a lot of borders in your
grounds haven't you ... How many borders would you say
you've got in your grounds?

MAN: I'm trying to read.

YOUNG MAN: Oh yes. I'm sorry. Don't let me disturb
you ... I'm not disturbing you am I ... I like reading
myself ... I read the dictionary a lot ... A very fine
book. Do you ever read it at all. An excellent book
for defining words. A definite key to our language ...

He looks out of the window.

You know I think we're going the wrong way ... I don't
recognise any of this countryside ... This train is going
to Manchester isn't it. This is the Manchester train ...

MAN: Yes.

YOUNG MAN: Well it's going the wrong way ... I don't
recognise any of this countryside ...

He starts to rise.

Do you think perhaps we should pull the
communication cord?

MAN: No, no ... Sit down.

YOUNG MAN: Someone should tell them. There's no
knowing where we'll end up if no one tells them.

MAN: Please sit down ... and leave that cord alone ...

YOUNG MAN: But I must get to Manchester.

MAN: Please calm yourself. Calm yourself ... Sit down ...
Sit down ... please ... This train is going to Manchester.

YOUNG MAN: Are you sure?

MAN: Yes, yes ... Now please sit down ...

YOUNG MAN: (*Starts to sit.*) These drivers can lose their way you know ... They're only working men ... They've got no university training ... They can lose their way.

MAN: I assure you this train is going to Manchester.

YOUNG MAN: Are you sure? They've got no maps up there you know ... There's no one qualified to read them that's the trouble ... There should be more people of university training employed on this work ... It's important that these trains should get to Manchester. What do you think? Don't you think I'm right. It's not the men's fault. I'm not blaming them. They're only working men ... It's the authorities ... Nothing is done to encourage men of learning to ride the footplate ... Men with degrees. You know where you are with men of degrees. They've got degrees and you know where you stand with them. That's why I wouldn't vote for these Labour people ... They haven't attempted to tackle this problem ... Nor have the others come to that ... That's why so many of these trains get lost. There's no one with navigational knowledge at the helm ...

He sits down.

I think it's important to have someone with navigational knowledge at the helm. That's where the Navy scores every time ... There's always someone with navigational knowledge at the helm in the Navy. They insist on it ... That's why they don't lose any of their ships ... You know I think the railways should be run by the Admiralty. We'd get decent people in command then. There'd be no more of this getting lost ... They'd put a qualified captain at the controls ... a full naval complement on the footplate. There'd be people up there then who could read maps ... and plot of course ... (*Pause.*) Are you sure

that case is not in your way up there ... (*Pause.*) You will
tell me if it is won't you ... (*Pause.*)

Then he starts to hum the tune of Mountain Greenery
*accompanied by banging his feet, and clicking his fingers,
and as he gets further carried away he makes drum noises
and cymbal sounds, and stamps his feet ... he finally stops.*

You ever been to a Jazz Club? Pretty good they are.
You hear some good music down them. I went to that
big festival at Beaulieu ... I think Jazz is an art form
don't you ... I used to play the drums once ... I was
very good. People said I was very good. I thought
about taking it up as a career. I even bought some
drums. Good ones they were ... Silver glitter shells,
dual snares, zildian cymbals ... tunable tom toms ...
I had three tunable tom toms ... I was getting on all
right with them. Some chaps I knew had formed this
band and we used to play at dances ... I was doing all
right ... Then I got this pain in my head ... Terrible
pain it was ... I couldn't hear with it ... My mum said
it was playing the drums did it. Well I had to go away
you see ... and while I was gone she sold my drums ...
I might have gone on playing the drums if she hadn't
sold them ... Because when I came back the pain was
gone. They got rid of the pain for me ... But the drums
were gone ... Still I might get some more one day ...
If this job goes all right ... I'm going after a job in
Manchester ... That's why I don't want this train to get
lost ... I must get there ... But if this job goes all right
I'll get some more drums ... you can get them on hire
purchase can't you ...

He looks out of the window.

I think we're going the right way now ... I recognise
some of this country ...

He continues to look out of the window and gradually takes up the train rhythm.

Tickety tum tickety tum tickety tum tickety tum.

He turns back from the window still making the rhythm and starts to study the other man. The YOUNG MAN starts to study the other MAN, very intently, rather as an artist would study a subject ... the MAN begins to get very uncomfortable ... The YOUNG MAN studies the front of his face, his profile, he squirms round on his seat to study the other profile ... finally he speaks.

Do you know something?

The MAN looks up at him.

You're very important aren't you? I would say to look at you, you're very important. Expensive suit, good material, well tailored, freshly clean white laundered shirt, nice tie ... Yes I would say to look at you you're very important ... It shows on your face. You've got an important looking face. Not like me. You wouldn't say that my face was important looking would you ... Would you? Would you say my face was important looking?

MAN: (*Embarrassed.*) I don't know. I really don't know ...

He hides behind his paper.

YOUNG MAN: No I don't think you would. I don't think anyone would ... It's because it's not important looking I suppose ... My face is not important looking at all is it? I wish it was sometimes. It's an asset to have an important looking face ... It helps you to get on ... Holds you back if you haven't got one. I've been held back lots of times just because of my face ... You go after a job and they don't like your face ... They always interview you when you go after a job ... That's

the idea ... so they can have a look at your face ...
And if it doesn't fit ... If your face doesn't fit you've
had it ...It's strange isn't it. How important your face
is ... It's only by your face that people recognise you
isn't it ... It's only by your face that I know it's you
sitting opposite me and not someone else ... If I saw
you again somewhere else I'd say hello I know that
face. It's funny that isn't. How we can only tell each
other by our faces. That's why it's so important to
have a good face ...

*During this last dialogue he gets up from his seat and
sits alongside the other MAN and studies his face more
closely.*

You've got a good face. (*Looks hard at it.*) Yes I would
say you've got a very good face. A very impressive
face. A professional face. Yes I would say you were
a professional man. Are you a professional man? You
are aren't you? You are a professional man. Why don't
you answer? Shy? Are you shy? (*Looks hard at him.*)
You are shy aren't you? I can see you are. You look
embarrassed. Ha ha fancy that. Fancy you being shy.
With all that professional face as well ... that good
suit ... all that bearing ... and underneath it all you're
shy ...Ha ha ... That's good that is ... That's very funny.

MAN: Will you be quiet. Go and sit in your own seat ...
(*He reaches for his brief case.*) I've got work to do ...

He opens it and starts to take papers out of it.

YOUNG MAN: My seat? Which is my seat? Eh? Which
seat is mine?

MAN: Please be quiet.

*He starts to read papers. He has a pen and he marks them
as he is reading them.*

YOUNG MAN: No. You've raised a question. You said to me go and sit in your own seat ... I'd like to know which is my seat. Eh? Which is my own seat?

MAN: Leave me alone.

YOUNG MAN: I'm not touching you. I've not touched you. Have I touched you? Are you inferring that I've touched you.

MAN: Stop bothering me. Please stop bothering me.

YOUNG MAN: I'm not bothering you. It's not me that's bothering you ... You're bothering me. That's the real truth of the matter. You're bothering me ... You don't want to think just because you're important looking you can take liberties you know. I might not be so unimportant as I look you know. I might be important too! ... You don't know me do you? You don't know who I am ... How do you know who I am. You want to be careful who you pick on.

MAN: (*Annoyed.*) Don't be foolish ... Please! I haven't said a word to you since you got in this carriage.

YOUNG MAN: I know you haven't. Not one single word. You've completely ignored me. Completely gone out of your way to ignore me ...

The MAN goes to speak.

Is that polite ... Is that friendly ... To go out of your way to completely ignore someone. Who do you think you are? Eh! Who do you think you are to completely ignore me ... eh? To go out of your way to do it? Eh? Who do you think you are?

MAN: I didn't ignore you ... I didn't go out of my way to completely ignore you ... I just didn't talk that's all.

YOUNG MAN: I know you didn't talk ... that's what I say ... You've hardly spoke one word to me since I got in this carriage.

MAN: I don't want to talk to you. Don't you understand. I don't want to talk to you.

YOUNG MAN: Why not! Why don't you want to talk to me. What reason have you got for not wanting to talk to me.

MAN: No reason. I just don't want to talk to you that's all.

YOUNG MAN: Oh no reason. I shouldn't think you would have any reason. Why should you have reasons for not wanting to talk to me ... You've never met me before ... I'm a complete stranger to you ...so why should you have reasons for not wanting to talk to me? You don't know me ... You've got nothing against me have you ... You haven't heard anything against me have you? Have you heard anything against me? (*Pause.*) Well answer me ... Have you ... Have you heard anything against me?

MAN: Of course I haven't. You know I haven't. How could I.

YOUNG MAN: Well why don't you want to talk to me.

MAN: (*Looks baffled.*) It's not you ... I ... It's not you. It's not just you that I don't want to talk to ... I ... don't want to talk to anyone.

YOUNG MAN: Not anyone?

MAN: No, not anyone.

YOUNG MAN: Not even your wife?

MAN: I'm not married ... Oh please.

YOUNG MAN: What about your mother ... Don't you want to talk to your mother.

MAN: My mother's not here is she ... How can I talk to my mother ... she's not here.

YOUNG MAN: If she was ... If she was here ... wouldn't you want to talk to her then?

The MAN looks around wildly for some way of escape.

Wouldn't you? Your own mother. The woman who brought you into the world ...

The MAN doesn't answer.

Well I must say that's a fine way to treat your mother. A marvelous way to treat her. Haven't you got any feelings for her at all? You interest me you know. People like you interest me. I bet you went to a good school, got a good start in life ... come from a good home ... all at your parents' expense ...Got on ... Yes ... made good in the world ... Got a nice big house now ... big garden ... with borders all round it ... all at your parents' expense ... But now you've got no feelings for them. You don't want to talk to them. If your own mother was in this carriage ... sitting in this carriage ... you wouldn't want to talk to her ... How do you think she'd feel ... sitting here in this carriage ... with her own son ... and he won't talk to her ...

MAN: Look I love my mother ... I think the world of her ... Now will you please shut up!!

YOUNG MAN: Oh you love her ... think the world of her ... Yet you won't talk to her ... That's a funny way to show it isn't it ...

MAN: Look will you please leave me alone ... I ... I don't know who you are, or what you are, or what you're at ...

but ... please leave me alone ... I've got a lot of work to do ... I don't want to be offensive ... but I'm entitled to privacy. I don't have to put up with you. I'm entitled to be left alone ... Look if you don't stop bothering me I ... I shall call the guard.

YOUNG MAN: Oh so you're going to call the guard are you? And how are you going to do that ...

The MAN's eyes go the communication cord ... and the YOUNG MAN's eyes follow them.

You're going to pull that cord are you? Stop the train ... inconvenience all the other passengers ... Just because you don't want to share this carriage with me ... Who do you think you are? You must think you're very important. Eh? I bet you must think you're pretty big ... Stop the train ... Call the guard ... just because someone else is riding in your carriage with you. Who are you? Who are you King of? You rich people make me laugh ... You think just because you've got a few pounds in the bank you own the earth ... You'll be shot you know ... When the revolution comes you'll be shot you know ... I suppose you know that ... You'll be one of the first to go ... People like you ...

MAN: (*Lets air escape through his teeth testily.*) Terrsse.

YOUNG MAN: Don't tersss me ... I'm not here to be terrssed ... I'm not a serf you know ... You don't frighten me with your important looking face ... and your terrsse ... If you wanted a carriage to yourself ... you should have picked one ... You should have picked an empty carriage ... There's plenty of them you know ... This train is not very full ... There's plenty of empty carriages ...

MAN: I did pick an empty carriage.

YOUNG MAN: But it's not an empty carriage. I'm in it.

MAN: Yes.

YOUNG MAN: And you ... You're in it too ... It can't be empty if we're in it can it ... Do you follow my logic? This is very interesting you know ... I find this very interesting ... Here we have an empty carriage ... or we did have if we're going to be logical ... Yes let's be logical ... Here we had an empty carriage ... You came along and tried to bag it for yourself ... All to yourself ... Then I came along and intruded on you ... Yes ... I'm an intruder aren't I ... I've got a ticket same as you ... but I'm an intruder ... I've invaded your privacy ... I'm sorry. I'm terribly sorry ... Your Highness I never saw the notices on the door ... Reserved for his Royal Highness ... King Kong ... Perhaps you'd like me to open the window and jump out ...

He opens the window.

Anything to oblige your Highness.

The wind blows in and the MAN's papers start to blow about ... he grabs them.

MAN: Shut that window! (*He shuts it.*)

YOUNG MAN: (*Opens it.*) No ... I want it open.

MAN: (*Shuts it.*) I want it shut ...

YOUNG MAN: (*Opens it.*) I want it open. (*He is treating it as a jest ... enjoying it very much.*)

MAN: (*Shuts it.*) Please will you keep it shut.

YOUNG MAN: No ...

He goes to open it ... but the man is standing in the way.

I'm going to open it ... Mind ...

MAN: No.

YOUNG MAN: It's my turn ... Come on play the game properly ... You've had your turn ...

The MAN doesn't move.

Look I've got as much right to have the window open as you have to keep it shut ... Or don't you recognise that right ... I suppose you don't recognise my rights ... I've got rights too you know ... I'll toss you for it ... Come on, heads it stays shut, tails it's open.

MAN: No ...

YOUNG MAN: You're not a sportsman are you ... All right ... You keep that one shut ...and I'll keep this one open ...

He goes to the other window and opens it.

There you are ... now we're even.

MAN: Shut that window ...

YOUNG MAN: No ... I shan't.

MAN: (*Furious.*) Shut that window.

YOUNG MAN: No.

The MAN glares at him furiously not knowing how to deal with him.

MAN: You ... You're a pest.

YOUNG MAN: It's no good you getting nasty ... You don't want to get nasty you know ... I've got as much right to have my window open as you have to keep yours shut ... Look I don't want to be unfriendly ... We don't want an ugly scene. I hate scenes ... I'll compromise with you ... That's the best way. Let's make a compromise. I'll shut my window if you'll open yours ...

The MAN sits down seething with rage, and goes back to his papers ... as he marks them he uses the pen rather savagely.

I suppose you think I'm being unreasonable don't you ... Just because I've got this window open you think I'm being unreasonable don't you ...

MAN: Yes I do.

YOUNG MAN: Well I think you're unreasonable for having yours shut ... It's just as unreasonable to have a window shut as it is to have it open you know ... Ah that's shut you up hasn't it ... That's taken the wind out of your sails ... You're lost for words now aren't you ... eh? It's always the same with you windbags ... You've plenty of old chat ... until you're faced with a piece of logic ... Get a few facts thrown at you and you don't know how to deal with them ... You're too abstract that's your trouble you know. Too much old fantasy ... Well you don't want to come the old fantasy with me you know ... You've picked the wrong bloke ... The old fantasia won't wash with me you know mate ...

While he has been talking the man has fished a cigarette out and is lighting it rather nervously.

Put that cigarette out while I'm talking to you.

MAN: Eh?

YOUNG MAN: (*Menacingly.*) Put that cigarette out.

MAN: What's it ... Eh ... No.

YOUNG MAN: Are you going to put that cigarette out when you're told, or have I got to make you.

He starts to move slowly towards the MAN.

The MAN starts to rise apprehensively.

MAN: Don't you come near me ... I'm warning you ...

YOUNG MAN: You're warning me? No ... I think you've got the wrong end of the stick old mate ... It's me that's warning you ... I'm the one that's doing the warning.

He comes nearer.

MAN: (*Backing away.*) I'm warning you ...

YOUNG MAN: You're not ... You're not warning me ... It's me that's warning you ... don't you understand I'm the one that's doing the warning ... I said it first ... stop using my words ... Use your own words ... Haven't you got any words of your own? Eh? Haven't you?

The MAN starts to reach for the communication cord.

YOUNG MAN: Don't touch that cord ... If you touch that cord I'll shoot.

The MAN looks alarmed and starts.

Ah, that's startled you ... You didn't know I had a gun did you.

He takes a revolver out of his pocket and shows it.

That's frightened you hasn't it ... It's funny the way people are frightened of guns isn't it? That's another fact I've observed, another little piece of logic ... You should observe facts you know ... They're very interesting ...

He suddenly springs up and puts the gun to the MAN's temple.

Now ... let's have a little chat ... Ha ha ... It's me that's important now isn't it ... it ... I'm the important one now aren't I ... Sit down ...

The MAN sits down and the YOUNG MAN sits beside him ... still with the gun pressed to the MAN's temple ... and he keeps it there all through the following dialogue ...

Now put that cigarette out ...

The MAN puts it out.

Why are you smoking?

MAN: I ... I'm sorry ...

YOUNG MAN: You're sorry. Why are you sorry ...
Are you sorry because you were smoking?

MAN: Yes.

YOUNG MAN: Why do you smoke then? Eh? Is it a
habit? Eh? It's a habit isn't it?

MAN: Yes.

YOUNG MAN: It's a nasty habit ... Isn't it ...It's a nasty
habit ...

MAN: Yes.

YOUNG MAN: Say it ... Say it's a nasty habit ...

MAN: It's a nasty habit ...

YOUNG MAN: Say smoking is a nasty habit ...

MAN: Smoking is a nasty habit ...

YOUNG MAN: And I want to give it up ... Go on say it ...
and I want to give it up.

MAN: And I want to give it up.

YOUNG MAN: Ah so you want to give it up ... So you
don't like smoking then.

MAN: Yes.

YOUNG MAN: Yes?

MAN: I mean no ...

YOUNG MAN: No? Yes and no ... You're not very explicit
are you? Are you?

MAN: No.

YOUNG MAN: Oh I see you agree with me ...

MAN: Yes.

YOUNG MAN: But I want you to be explicit. These are very important questions I'm asking you ... And I want very explicit answers ... I want these questions answered explicitly ... in a very explicit manner. Do you understand?

MAN: Yes.

YOUNG MAN: Well we'll start again then ... So you don't like smoking?

MAN: No.

YOUNG MAN: Why do you smoke then?

MAN: I ... Er ... It's a habit ...

YOUNG MAN: A habit? Hm ... And you can't give it up?

MAN: No.

YOUNG MAN: Have you tried?

MAN: Er no ...

YOUNG MAN: How do you know you can't give it up then?

MAN: I ...

YOUNG MAN: Let's try it now ... Let's see if you can give it up now ... Have you got any cigarettes?

MAN: Yes.

YOUNG MAN: Get them out ...

The MAN brings out a case.

Would you like to smoke a cigarette?

MAN: Er ...

YOUNG MAN: Well would you?

MAN: I er ...

YOUNG MAN: Well?

MAN: I don't know what to say.

YOUNG MAN: You must say what you think ...

The MAN looks out of the corner of his eye at the gun ...
He is very frightened and shows it.

You mustn't be frightened of the gun. It won't go
off unless I pull the trigger. Guns are quite inanimate
you know. They're inanimate objects. Well would
you like a cigarette? You would like a cigarette
wouldn't you.

MAN: Yes.

YOUNG MAN: You'd like one very much wouldn't you?

MAN: Yes.

YOUNG MAN: Well you can't have one ... (*Pause.*)
You haven't smoked one have you.

MAN: No.

YOUNG MAN: But you wanted to didn't you.

MAN: Yes.

YOUNG MAN: But you didn't smoke it.

MAN: No.

YOUNG MAN: There you are you see ... You've given it
up ... As easy as that ... Just put a gun to your head
and you give up smoking as easy as that ... (*Snaps his*
fingers.) You should have a gun put to your head more

often. It's very good for you. What other bad habits have you got. Perhaps we could cure you of a few more ... Eh? What other bad habits have you got?

MAN: I don't know.

YOUNG MAN: You don't know? You know I think you're being very deceitful ... There must be lots of bad habits you've got ... But you won't own up to them will you ... You want to keep them don't you ... Don't you ...

MAN: No ...

YOUNG MAN: I know of a very bad habit you've got ... You're unsociable. Aren't you ... You're very unsociable ... You won't talk to people ... You're a very bad travelling companion ... I wonder if we could make you a better travelling companion ... Let's try shall we? Let's have a singsong. Do you know *Mountain Greenery*?

MAN: No ...

YOUNG MAN: Oh you must know it ... Think ... (*Sings.*) Bah bah bah bar bar (*First few bars.*) You must know that one ...

MAN: No ...

YOUNG MAN: Well let's see if we can teach you it ... If you don't start singing it before I count ten ... I'm going to pull the trigger. One ... two ... three ... four.

The MAN starts to sing Mountain Greenery.

Marvellous ... Having a gun to your head really helps you doesn't it ... Look I tell you what we'll do ... We'll have a jazz session ... You make a saxophone noise ... and I'll make drum noises ... All right ... after four ... Ready ... One two three four ...

The MAN makes a saxophone noise and the YOUNG MAN makes the drum and cymbal noises he was making earlier on.

(*During it.*) Take it easy ... you're rushing ... You're speeding up ... Listen to the beat ... You're dragging ... Your tempo's all over the place ... Get with it man ... That's it ... crazy ... Blow ... Yeah blow ... blow blow man ... blow ... Now go on all on your own ... Go on, eight bars all on your own ...

The MAN makes sax noises for eight bars on his own with the YOUNG MAN making interjections.

Yeah ... Blow ... go go ... go ... blow ... blow man ... Yeah ... I dig you dadyo ... Yeah ... You're the greatest ...

The MAN comes to a stop.

That was a rave man. I dig you ... You're gone ... That was real swinging.

In his excitement he has let the gun drop down from the MAN's temple ... and he is not watching it ... the MAN suddenly springs and tries to grab it. But the YOUNG MAN is too quick for him ... and places it at his temple again after a short struggle for it.

Back ... Back ... So that's your game ... Can't be trusted eh? Just like a bloody dog you are ... just take your eyes off them for a minute and they're snapping at you ... That's it ... That's what you are a dog ... Bark ... go on ... bark ... bark.

The MAN makes a barking noise.

No, not like that ... You're not a Pekinese ... You're an Alsatian ... be an Alsatian ... go on, be an Alsatian ... Bark like an Alsatian ...

The MAN in his fear tries to do it.

Louder ... louder ... Down boy ... down ... down ...
Good dog ... that's a good dog ... Off the seat boy ...
I'll get into trouble if anyone sees you sitting on the
seat boy ... Dogs are not allowed on the seat ... On the
floor boy ... Down on the floor ...

MAN: No ... I won't.

YOUNG MAN: Down ... on the floor ... on the floor ...

The MAN gets down on the floor.

There's a good dog ...

He looks at him for a few seconds and his mood changes.

I'm fed up with this game ... All this skylarking about
... It's upset me ... My head's started to ache again ...

*He holds his head ... and the gun drops out of his hand onto
the floor ... the MAN grabs for it ... and jumps up with the
gun trained on the YOUNG MAN.*

MAN: You'll pay for this ... You're going to pay for this ...

*The YOUNG MAN doesn't answer. He sits with his head
in his hands.*

D'you hear ... you're going to pay for this ... I've got
the gun now ... See I've got it now ...

YOUNG MAN: You're welcome to it ...

MAN: Stand up.

YOUNG MAN: Eh?

MAN: I said stand up ... Stand up.

YOUNG MAN: Oh don't be daft.

MAN: Stand up ... Stand up ... I said.

YOUNG MAN: No. I don't want to stand up ... And I wish you'd keep your voice down ... my head aches ...

MAN: Stand up ... Look I've got the gun ... I said stand up ...

YOUNG MAN: Oh stop playing the fool ... You're getting on my nerves you are ... What time do we get into Manchester? We ought to be in Manchester soon didn't we ...

MAN: You're not going to get away with this you know ... I'm going to make you pay for this ...

YOUNG MAN: I haven't got any money ...

MAN: I'm not talking about money ... I'm going to hand you over to the police ... I'm going to hand you over ... as soon as we get to Manchester ...

YOUNG MAN: We should be there soon.

He looks at his watch.

What time do you make it ... I think I'm a bit slow ... We'd better get ready ... I think we're getting very close ...

MAN: I'm ready ...

YOUNG MAN: I'm not ... (*He goes to get his case.*)

MAN: Leave that case alone ...

The YOUNG MAN gets his case down

Leave that case alone ...

The YOUNG MAN ignores him and goes to open it.

Leave that case alone ...

YOUNG MAN: I've got to get some things out.

MAN: You said that case was empty ...

YOUNG MAN: It is, except for a few things ...

MAN: What's in it.

YOUNG MAN: Nothing ... It's empty.

MAN: You said you had some things in it ...

YOUNG MAN: Yes ... but apart from that it's empty.

He goes to open it.

MAN: Don't open it ...

YOUNG MAN: I've got to ... I want to get my things out ...

MAN: Leave it.

The YOUNG MAN opens the case and takes out an actor's make-up box ... from this he takes out a beard and spirit gum ... and puts the beard on and then some false eyebrows ... and a different nose ...

What are you doing?

YOUNG MAN: I'm getting ready.

MAN: Why are you putting that beard on ... What are you doing.

YOUNG MAN: I've got someone meeting me ...

The train pulls to a stop ...

FX: GRAMS. Disc. Band: Sound of station noises.

People start to walk past the window of the carriage ...

YOUNG MAN: (*Picks up his case.*) Ah we're well on time. (*He starts to open the carriage door.*)

MAN: Stop! You're not getting away with this ...

Threatens him again with the gun.

YOUNG MAN: (*Looks at gun and smiles.*) I suppose you know that's a toy gun.

MAN: Eh? ... (*Looks at it.*) Toy ...

YOUNG MAN: (*Confidingly, squeezing his arm.*) That's what toys are for ... to play with ... and we've had a lovely game ... Cheerio ...

The YOUNG MAN steps out of the carriage and walks away humming Mountain Greenery. *Stay on the MAN ... he stands looking stupidly at the toy gun ... as the music of* Mountain Greenery *swells up loud ... as it reaches its climax the MAN pulls the trigger and the gun makes a childish pop ...*

Fade out.

THE KNACKER'S YARD

The Knacker's Yard was first performed at the Arts Theatre on the 16th January 1962. It was directed by Alan Simpson, with the following cast:

RYDER, Maxwell Shaw

MARTIN, Dermot Kelly

SOPHIA, Margie Lawrence

1st POLICEMAN, Richard Klee

2nd POLICEMAN, Brian Jackson

Directed by Alan Simpson

Produced by A.L.S. Presentations Ltd., by arrangements with the Arts Theatre

ACT ONE

Scene One

A room. A window in the far wall, the bottom half covered by an old and dirty piece of curtaining. A crack in one of the panes. And a piece of brown paper replacing another. An old iron bedstead, probably ex-hospital stock, stands against one wall. A thin narrow cupboard, very badly painted with a thin coat of undercoat in off-white, covering what was once brown, stands near the bed. One small threadbare piece of carpet covers a few of the bare boards. A very ancient gas stove stands in one corner. All round the area, is covered with grease and dirty cooking stains. A pot and a kettle stand on it. In another corner is an old sink. A folding table stands in the middle of the room. The room is in darkness and is lit only by a thin stream of moonlight shining through the dirty window. After a pause of some minutes, enabling the audience to drink in the scene, footsteps and voices are heard off. RYDER's room occupies about two thirds of the stage. The other third is the landing, with doors off leading to various rooms... one of these rooms is MARTIN's. To the back of the stage, on the part that is the landing, can be seen the head of the stairs leading down. These should be practical so that the characters can enter and exit by them.

SOPHIA: Mind that step there... there's a loose board... I keep asking Ellis to mend that... He won't though... Someone's got to kill themselves 'fore he'll put a nail in it.

RYDER and SOPHIA appear at head of stairs and walk towards one of the rooms...

SOPHIA: That's the way he works – He works that way. He'd let the house fall about him he would... 'fore he'd put a nail in a loose board. Mind, there's another one up there... Makes them dangerous, this landing being dark...

RYDER: Isn't there a light?

SOPHIA: Yes... but he won't put no bulbs in them... Some of the tenants was willing to put bulbs in them... but he's

93

had the wires cut. That's the way he works. He says it's too expensive with lights burning all over the landings ... It is expensive, running a boarding house these days. There ain't no money in it. They won't pay the money for the rooms... That's the trouble... It takes all your time to get the money for the rooms.

By this time the door to the room has opened and we can see them in shadow standing at the entrance of the room.

SOPHIA: I think there's a bulb in this room...

She flicks the switch and the room lights up. The bulb is suspended from a length of cord hanging from the ceiling. It is uncovered and very dusty. SOPHIA is a woman of indeterminate age, perhaps fortyish. Still reasonably slim figured. She is heavily made up, in a revolting way, and wears a cheap dress of modern style, and has her hair brassly waved. RYDER is wearing a old suit that is patched in various places and exaggeratedly pressed. His suit is of modern styling. He is a youngish man. He carries two suitcases which he puts down.

SOPHIA: There we are. I hope you'll like it. We try to make the rooms cosy. It's quite cosy this one... don't you think? Self-contained and cosy... There's a new pane being put in there... I've seen Ellis about it... He cuts down on the landings... but he's not stingy in the rooms... I'll say that for him... He'll put a new pane in there alright... Won't be for a few weeks... he'll see if you stay first... no good making the room cosy if you ain't going to stay...

RYDER is looking round the room. He is obviously not very impressed by it.

SOPHIA: You are going to stay are you? You didn't say in your letter how long you wanted the room for... I suppose it'll be for a few weeks... be a few weeks I suppose won't it...

RYDER: I don't know. I might stay longer... I might stay a long time.

SOPHIA: Suppose it depends does it?

RYDER: Yes... it depends.

SOPHIA: Suppose you don't know?

RYDER: I move about a lot. I'm thinking about staying put though. I want to get a place.

SOPHIA: You need a place. Everyone needs a place. You want roots. Somewhere to come back to.

RYDER: Yes – I'd like to get a place. (*He goes over to gas stove.*) This work?

SOPHIA: Yes... the knobs... you turn the knobs.

RYDER: I know. It works then, eh?

SOPHIA: Needs money in it... there's a box in the corner. If you want a shilling, I've always got plenty of shillings. Ellis opens the box. He's got a key.

RYDER: It's not the Gas Company then?

SOPHIA: No it's Ellis. Ellis does all that. He's got an arrangement.

RYDER looks at it... lifts the kettle... looks inside it...

SOPHIA: I suppose you don't know then?

RYDER: What?

SOPHIA: How long you'll be here?

RYDER: It's safe is it?

SOPHIA: Only, if you know how long... it'd help us you see – we don't like these rooms to be empty... if you see what I mean... especially with everyone after them...

RYDER: No... of course not... (*He looks in the pot.*)

SOPHIA: It's better if you stay long. The longer you stay the better it is.

RYDER: Who for?

SOPHIA: Eh?

RYDER: You said the better it is... who for?

SOPHIA: For you. Ellis prefers residentials... he helps them. He adjusts the terms. I mean you're better off with adjusted terms aren't you?

RYDER opens the door and looks inside.

RYDER: Just big enough to put your head in...

SOPHIA: It's not every place gives adjusted terms... but Ellis likes residentials...

RYDER: (*Shuts the oven door.*) Do you get much of that?

SOPHIA: What?

RYDER: People sticking their heads in the oven.

SOPHIA: Sticking their heads in the oven?

RYDER: People do it. They do it all the time. You read about it in the papers... found in locked rooms with their head in the oven... suicides... you read about it all the time. Saw a chap this morning... was going to chuck himself under a train at Farringdon... there's a lot of it goes on. Do you get much of it here?

SOPHIA: People gassing themselves... (*Laughs.*) You're a funny one you are... What put that in your head?

RYDER: (*Indicates gas stove.*) Handy... That's handy for that sort of thing... Nice size.

SOPHIA: You've got some funny ideas you have.

RYDER: (*Looks in the pot again.*) This pot's dirty.

SOPHIA: That's got to be cleaned.

RYDER: What's it had in it?

SOPHIA: What, in there...?

RYDER: Yes...

She looks.

SOPHIA: What is it?

RYDER: Dunno... some muck...

SOPHIA: They were foreigners had this room.

RYDER: Same stuff in the kettle. (*She looks.*)

SOPHIA: What is it...?

RYDER: Muck of some sort.

SOPHIA: It's muck alright... It's got to be cleaned though
that 'as – I don't like to see dirty things in a room –
I like things spotless – I always say it doesn't cost much
to be clean – It's just getting the time, that's all.

RYDER: No. (*He goes over to the table.*)

SOPHIA: I suppose you don't know how long you'll be
staying then?

RYDER: This is dirty too.

SOPHIA: Only if you had any idea... It would help you
see... It'd help us with our planning – You've got to plan
in a place like this.

RYDER: Did you say they were foreigners had this room?

SOPHIA: Yes... man and a woman... both foreigners.

RYDER: Both of them?

SOPHIA: Yes. We didn't want them to have it. Ellis don't like foreigners. He'd rather have someone English any day. But they paid extra you see. That's the only good thing about foreigners... they always pay extra. Ellis wouldn't take them otherwise. He hates having foreigners in the house. It's funny that... him not liking foreigners... 'cos he's not English himself...

RYDER: What is he? What nationality is he?

SOPHIA: Who, Ellis?... I don't know. He's not English. I think he used to be an Indian... He's dark like they are.

RYDER: Indian? Hm... And he don't like foreigners...

SOPHIA: No. He hates them.

RYDER: Were they married?

SOPHIA: Who?

RYDER: The foreigners.

SOPHIA: I don't know. We never spoke to them. Well, you don't want to get too familiar do you?

RYDER: They were dirty...

SOPHIA: Eh?

RYDER: They weren't very clean.

SOPHIA: No, well you can't expect it can you, where they came from they're not brought up to it are they – that pot proves it...

RYDER: And the sink.

SOPHIA: That kettle too... (*She looks in it.*) What is it?

RYDER: Don't know... some muck... some muck they've had...

SOPHIA: It's for water, this kettle... supposed to be for
water... not putting this sort of stuff in.

RYDER: When are you going to clean them then?

SOPHIA: Oh, it'll be done... It'll be done alright... don't
worry... Do you like the room?

RYDER: It's not what I'm used to.

SOPHIA: No – It could be made to look nice, couldn't it?

RYDER: If I'm going to stay I'd like some alterations.
I'd expect some alterations done.

SOPHIA: Oh, you're thinking of staying then, are you?

RYDER: Well, I need a place... I definitely need a place.

SOPHIA: Well, it's cosy... I mean, it's nice and cosy...
I mean all you need is a few little bits and pieces of
your own in here and it'd soon start looking something...

RYDER: You couldn't expect me to live in it as it is...
I'd want things done... It wouldn't suit as it is... I'd need
a lamp shade... That's something I'd need right away...

SOPHIA: Oh, you could have that. You could have
that alright. Ellis has been thinking about putting
lamp shades in all the rooms... He wants to make
improvements... He's been thinking about improvements
for a long time...

RYDER: Yes, well I'd want that.

SOPHIA: You could have it... We're quite willing to make
those sort of improvements.

RYDER: You'd need a lamp in this room...

SOPHIA: I suppose you don't know how long... You don't
know how long then...

RYDER: No... It depends...

SOPHIA: Ellis would have to know... If he's got to do improvements... he'd have to know...

RYDER: I have to keep moving... that's my trouble... that's about the size of it...

SOPHIA: Can't you settle?

RYDER: I could settle... If I didn't have to keep moving... I could settle then alright...

SOPHIA: Hm, he'd have to know. Ellis'd have to know...

RYDER walks round the room... looking at things.

RYDER: I'd let him know... I'd keep him informed... I want a place... This could be my set-up... It's ideal... This'd fit me... I think this'd fit...

SOPHIA: It's cosy... The lamp shade would make it look very cosy.

RYDER: I'd need that... I'd definitely need that...

He continues to look round... sizing the place up... She watches him.

RYDER: There's no chair.

SOPHIA: It's got a bed – you could sit on the bed.

RYDER: I'd need a chair.

SOPHIA: We could get you one... Ellis'd fit you up... He'd see you got a chair...

RYDER: What sort of chair?

SOPHIA: A nice one, we'd get one you liked. He'd do that alright...

RYDER: And these utensils?

SOPHIA: They'd be cleaned... We'd get them cleaned...

RYDER: And adjusted terms?

SOPHIA: And no interference.

RYDER: No interference?

SOPHIA: Not if you're a residential... You can do what you like... anything you want to do... you can do it...

RYDER: What can I do?

SOPHIA: Anything you want... if you want to do it... you can... You can do it... If you get what I mean... There'd be no interference... no questions asked.

RYDER: What sort of questions?

SOPHIA: None... There wouldn't be any asked at all... Not if you were residential...

RYDER: Why should there be any questions asked?

SOPHIA: There wouldn't be... That's what I'm saying... You wouldn't be asked any... There'd be no interference at all... None... You could do what you wanted.

RYDER: That's guaranteed, is it?

SOPHIA: Yes.

RYDER: It'd be in the contract?

SOPHIA: He'd put in a clause.

RYDER: He'd put a clause in it would he?

SOPHIA: He'd put in a clause...

RYDER: I'm not struck on contracts... I don't like contracts. If you know what I mean... They're too binding... They bind you down too much... I don't want to be restricted. You sign a contract... and before you know where you are you're contracted... You're tied up... Bound down and tied up... It's not what I want you see... I've always fought shy of that sort of thing...

SOPHIA: You wouldn't be tied down... It wouldn't bind you... or tie you up... Ellis wouldn't do that... It's not the way he works.

RYDER: It'd be a contract though.

SOPHIA: Not a binding one.

RYDER: It'd have clauses though...

SOPHIA: Nothing binding... It wouldn't tie you.

RYDER: That's guaranteed is it?

SOPHIA: Yes...

RYDER: It'd be in the contract?

SOPHIA: He'd put in a clause.

RYDER: A nullifying clause?

SOPHIA: Yes... that's the way Ellis works.

RYDER: He'd expect me to sign it though?

SOPHIA: Not if you didn't want to.

RYDER: Alright... Get him to make it out.

SOPHIA: I'll get him to do it.

Pause.

SOPHIA: How long then?

RYDER: What?

SOPHIA: The room... How long? Could you let us know how long?

RYDER: I'll have to think about it. Tell him I'll think about it. Tell him I like it... But I've got to think about it... I've got to work it out... I've got to see how my business fits in you see. I'd have to be able to conduct that... You've got no objections have you?

SOPHIA: What?

RYDER: To that... conducting my business... I'd have to conduct it you see... from here... You wouldn't mind that?

SOPHIA: What is your business?

RYDER: Well, that's a personal matter... I don't want to discuss that. Not at this stage.

SOPHIA: He'd have to know. Ellis'd have to know.

RYDER: You said there'd be no questions.

SOPHIA: There won't be... not if you're residential.

RYDER: I'm residential... You can put down for adjusted terms.

SOPHIA: I'll tell Ellis...

RYDER: Yes, you can tell him that... and no questions.

SOPHIA: No questions. (*She goes to the door. As she opens it we hear loud barking of lots of dogs.*)

RYDER: What's that?

SOPHIA: Dogs.

RYDER: Dogs?

SOPHIA: Yes... they always bark like that. You can't stop them. Ellis has tried... He can't stop them. They always bark like that.

RYDER: Where does he keep them?

SOPHIA: What?

RYDER: All those dogs... Where does he keep them?

SOPHIA: In the cellar.

RYDER: In the cellar...

SOPHIA: In hutches in the cellar... He loves dogs... If he sees any in the street... any stray dogs... he brings them home. He's got a cellar full.

A door shuts downstairs and the barking stops.

SOPHIA: That's what all that wood is out in the yard. He's got to make some more hutches for them.

RYDER: He keeps all those dogs... in hutches... in the cellar...

SOPHIA: Yes, he's very kind to dogs. He thinks the world of dogs... He'd sooner help dogs than human beings any day.

RYDER: How many's he got down there?

SOPHIA: I don't know. About fifty... sixty... I haven't counted them. He's getting full up down there. He was saying the other day... he's getting full up down there... He's been thinking about using one of the rooms...

RYDER: Doesn't anyone complain?

SOPHIA: About what?

RYDER: The dogs... about the dogs... They make a din... They must make a din.

SOPHIA: Some of them get up petitions. There's been some petitions got up... but no one signs them. No point, is there... You can't stop dogs barking. It's natural for them to bark. You've never heard a dog that didn't bark. I'll fix that chair for you.

*She goes and shuts the door. RYDER stands there for a second, then
runs to the door and opens it.*

RYDER: I say... You!

SOPHIA: (*Off.*) Me?

RYDER: Yes... What's your name?

SOPHIA: Sophia. (*She comes back into the doorway.*)

RYDER: Sophia.

SOPHIA: Yes... It's a nice name isn't it?

RYDER: Yes... It's alright... yes.

SOPHIA: Do you like it?

RYDER: I dunno... I'll think about it. Can I think about it?

SOPHIA: Yes... I think you'll like it. Most people do.

RYDER: Yes... I've got a thing about names, though...
    I either like them or I don't.

SOPHIA: Do you like mine?

RYDER: I'll think about it. A name takes time. I like to
    think about them.

SOPHIA: What did you want?

RYDER: Eh?

SOPHIA: You called me back...

RYDER: Oh, yes... Yes, I did... I did call you back didn't I.
    (*Pause.*) The lampshade... You won't forget the lampshade,
    will you?

SOPHIA: No. I'll see about it... and the chair... I'll see Ellis
    now. (*She goes out and RYDER shuts the door.*)

RYDER: She must be mad... raving mad... potty... she thinks
    I'm going to sign any contracts... (*He picks up one of his cases*

and puts it on the bed and opens it.) Sign a contract like that... you could spent the rest of your life here... (*He takes a pin-up picture out of his case and proceeds to pin it on the wall.*) They're very clever with their contracts... some of these people... they could have a clause in there... bind you right down... tie you up and you couldn't move. (*He stands back to admire the picture and starts to put another one up. In all he puts up about ten of them... very revealing pin-ups... in a line he puts them and above this line of pin-ups he puts a picture of the QUEEN and PRINCE PHILIP and a family group including the CHILDREN.*) Oh, no... I'm not signing any of their contracts. They won't catch me on that one... Get your name on the bottom of one of them... and they've got you tied up for life. Seen too much of that... Oh, no... they won't catch me as easy as that. I bet she thinks she's pretty smart, eh? Her and that Ellis... trying that on me... (*He stands back to admire the pictures. Then he takes his coat and trousers off, hangs them on a hanger and puts them in the cupboard... which is rigged up as a wardrobe... He shuts the door and sits on the bed.*) They ought to have a chair in here. (*He sits staring for a little while, then he gets up and goes over to the stove again and looks in the kettle.*) I wonder what it is... Muck... some muck... that's what it is, alright... muck... foreign muck of some sort...

There is a knock on the door. He listens. The knock comes again... he tip-toes over to the door and listens with his ear to it... the knock comes again. He kneels down and peers through the keyhole. The knock comes again. He rises and puts his ear to the door.

RYDER: Who is it?

MARTIN: It's me.

RYDER: Who?

MARTIN: Me.

RYDER: Who's me?

MARTIN: Eh?

RYDER: Who are you? What's your name?

MARTIN: Martin. My name's Martin... I live here.

RYDER: What do you want?

MARTIN: I want to talk to you.

RYDER: What about?

MARTIN: Eh?

RYDER: What do you want to talk about?

MARTIN: Eh? I want to talk to you... I just want to talk to you that's all...

RYDER: What about?

MARTIN: Eh? Well... er... what do you mean? What's the matter? Open the door.

RYDER: Why should I open the door to you. This is my room. Why should I open the door. I don't know who you are.

MARTIN: Martin. I'm Martin.

RYDER: Who's Martin?

MARTIN: Eh?... I am. I'm Martin.

RYDER: That doesn't tell me anything... Anyone could be Martin. Martin could be anyone. That doesn't mean anything to me... Martin... That doesn't tell me anything.

MARTIN: Look, open the door. I want to talk to you... that's all. I only want to talk to you... It's alright...

RYDER: What's the game then? Why do you want to talk to me? Eh? What's the game?

MARTIN: Nothing... No game. I just want to talk to you, that's all.

RYDER: You're not Ellis are you?

MARTIN: No... I'm not Ellis. I'm Martin... I'm not Ellis.

RYDER: Where's Ellis?

MARTIN: He's downstairs feeding his dogs.

RYDER: Is he getting that lampshade?

MARTIN: What lampshade?

RYDER: My lampshade... He promised me a lampshade.

MARTIN: Eh? I don't know nothing about any lampshade.

Pause. RYDER stays listening with his ear to the door.

RYDER: What are you doing out there?

MARTIN: Nothing. Just waiting, that's all... just waiting...

RYDER: What for? What are you waiting for?

MARTIN: For you to open the door. You going to open it?

RYDER: How do I know you're not Ellis?

MARTIN: 'Cos I'm Martin. How can I be Ellis if I'm Martin.

RYDER: Ellis could say he was Martin. Nothing to stop him... He could say that... He could easy say that.

MARTIN: Ellis is not up here. He never comes up here.

RYDER: Why not?

MARTIN: He's frightened of the dark. He won't ever come up here... Ellis won't.

Pause.

MARTIN: You frightened of Ellis?

RYDER: Why should I be frightened of Ellis?

MARTIN: Open the door then...

RYDER stands there thinking for a while.

RYDER: Alright then. Don't go away.

He goes over to the cupboard and puts his suit on again, and then he unbolts the door and opens it. MARTIN sidles in. He looks all round the room.

MARTIN: Why wouldn't you open the door... You frightened... You frightened of someone?

RYDER: Why should I be frightened... Why should I be frightened of anyone?

MARTIN: Well, you get some people... some of them are frightened of anything... frightened of their shadow some of them.

RYDER: I'm not the nervous type.

MARTIN: You're not.

RYDER: No. Never have been. I can sleep in the dark. Windows open... doors unbolted... it doesn't bother me. Same during the war... I used to walk around without a tin hat on.

MARTIN: In the front line?

RYDER: Anywhere... doesn't bother me. I've been up in airplane. You ever been up in airplane?

MARTIN: No.

RYDER: You want to try it. Talk about frightened... If you're the nervous type... you want to try it. Doesn't bother me... flying... I've done it... doesn't bother me a bit.

MARTIN: Why were you wearing your underpants just now?

RYDER: Eh?

MARTIN: Why were you wearing your underpants?

RYDER: I always wear underpants.

MARTIN: But you wasn't wearing a suit... you wasn't wearing your suit just now.

RYDER: How do you know?

MARTIN: I saw you through the keyhole.

RYDER: Spying on me. You were spying on me. So that's your game. Spying on me, eh? (*He grabs him by the collar.*) Who put you up to that... eh? Who told you to do that?

MARTIN: I wasn't spying on you. Let go... You're choking me... Let go.

RYDER: Why were you spying on me?

MARTIN: I wasn't spying on you... I wasn't... Honest... I wasn't. It's the truth.

RYDER: What was you looking through the keyhole for then?

MARTIN: Just wanted to see what you were doing... that's all... Just wanted to see what you were doing... I wanted to see what you were like... I live here. I wanted to see what you was like that's all... you got to know who you're up against.

RYDER throws him and he falls to the ground.

RYDER: Don't let me catch you that's all. Don't let me catch you...

MARTIN: (*Feeling his neck.*) You've hurt my neck... you hurt my neck doing that...

110

RYDER: Get up... Get up.

MARTIN gets up.

RYDER: You still think I'm frightened... Eh? You still think I'm frightened?

MARTIN: (*Holding his throat.*) No.

RYDER: I'm not the nervous type mate... There's nothing nervous about me. What do you want? What did you come in here for?

MARTIN: Nothing.

RYDER: Nothing? You must have wanted something. What was it?

MARTIN: Nothing... honest... nothing.

RYDER: You trying to play games with me?

MARTIN: No... No, I'm not.

RYDER: What do you want then... People don't come knocking on people's doors for nothing. You didn't do all that knocking for nothing.

MARTIN: Yes.

RYDER: You are playing games then.

MARTIN: No.

RYDER: That's a game isn't it...? Knocking on people's doors for nothing. That's a game... knocking down Ginger... I used to play it... I used to play it as a kid. It's a kid's game. It's a bit different, though, when grown men play it. I don't think I like it when grown men play it... Not on my door... Especially when they play it on my door.

MARTIN: I wasn't playing that... I wasn't doing that.

RYDER: What did you want then? Eh? What did you want?

MARTIN: I wanted to talk to you.

RYDER: Talk to me. What about? What did you want to talk to me about?

MARTIN: I ain't had nothing to eat all day... I thought perhaps... I thought you might have a bit of food... something you didn't want. People don't eat all their dinner... I thought perhaps... I ain't had nothing to eat you see. Nothing to eat all day. I won't get nothing tonight either.

Pause.

MARTIN: Not a thing I ain't had. Nothing. All day without nothing I been.

Pause.

MARTIN: No breakfast I ain't had. No dinner. I ought to kill myself.

RYDER: I saw you on the station this morning, didn't I?

MARTIN: Eh?

RYDER: You. I saw you on the station this morning.

MARTIN: What?

RYDER: Paddington tube station. I saw you there this morning. On the platform. You were saying all that then. You were going to jump under a train, you said.

MARTIN: I was. Yes. I was. The bloody thing didn't come in, though. Bleeding railways. You get all ready to do it. You're going to do it. And then the bleeding train don't come in.

RYDER: I thought you were going to do it.

MARTIN: I was. Yes, I was. I was going to do it alright.

RYDER: You didn't, though. Did you?

MARTIN: I told you the bleeding train...

RYDER: I stood and watched you. I missed my train watching you.

MARTIN: Eh?

RYDER: I thought you meant it. I thought you were serious. You looked serious.

MARTIN: What? I was. I was serious.

RYDER: Four trains come in while I stood there.

MARTIN: Eh? What? You don't think you jump under the first train that comes in, do you? Eh? That wants a bit of working up to. Eh? You don't go and buy a bleeding platform ticket and jump under the first train, you know. Jumping under trains ain't like catching 'em, you know. You ain't in that bleeding hurry, are you? Go jumping under trains like that. We ain't all bleeding heros, you know.

RYDER: Why do you swear so much?

MARTIN: Eh? Who swears?

RYDER: You do. You swear.

MARTIN: Who does?

RYDER: You do.

MARTIN: Who me?

RYDER looks pointedly round the room, peers into corners and then looks under the bed.

MARTIN: What are you looking for?

RYDER: I'm looking to see who you might think I'm talking to.

MARTIN: Eh? Who?... You're talking to me... ain't you?

RYDER: That's what I thought.

MARTIN: Eh? Here, what's going on?

RYDER: I don't know. You tell me. I'm talking to you. And you keep saying to me – who me? So I'm wondering if there might be someone else here you think I'm talking to.

MARTIN: Eh? There's no one else here. (*Looking round.*)

RYDER: I know.

MARTIN: What are you looking for then?

RYDER: You're not very bright, are you?

MARTIN: Eh? You taking the piss out of me?

RYDER: There you go again.

MARTIN: What?

RYDER: Swearing. Nearly every other word.

MARTIN: Eh? What are you... You one of them bleeding churchgoers... or something?

RYDER: No. No, I'm not one of them bleeding churchgoers... I'm not bloody anything... and I'm not very bloody keen on your bloody swearing! So bloody well shut it!!

MARTIN: You don't want to go picking holes in me, matey. You don't want to go picking holes in me. What I does is my affair. Eh? What I does is my affair... If I want to swear, eh? That's my business, an' it.

RYDER: You want to make something out of it?

MARTIN: Eh?

RYDER: Do you want to make something out of it?

MARTIN: What?

RYDER: You've got a marvellous command of language, haven't you? Are you a linguist?

MARTIN: What...

RYDER: There you go again. What... eh... what... Are they the only two words you know? I used to know a chap like you in Manchester. Complete ignoramus he was... just like you... No brain at all to speak of. A dirty stinking little wretch. Used to spend all his time ferreting a round dustbins.

MARTIN: I don't ferret around no dustbins.

RYDER: Why not? Why don't you? You want food, don't you? Too proud, I suppose... too proud for that, eh?

MARTIN: I'm not a tramp.

RYDER: A snob too. You know, you ought to go and see a psychologist. I'll make an appointment with mine if you like. One of the best, he is. He straightened me out.

MARTIN: I dunno... I dunno if I hold in with them... I dunno... I knew a bloke went to see one of them... and he ended up in the nut house... Just for seeing one of them... I dunno... I don't think I hold in with that. I say... let well alone, I say.

RYDER: You mustn't refuse medical aid. Some of those men spend all their lives studying medicine, you know. They don't do it for nothing. You mustn't waste their time, you know.

MARTIN: I'm not wasting their time.

RYDER: Yes you are... you're wasting their time.

MARTIN: (*Indignant.*) I've not been to see none of them.

RYDER: That's a waste. That's what I'm telling you. You're
wasting their time... There they are... They've spent years
studying... to help people like you... and you won't go and
see them. That's a waste. (*He becomes very emotional.*) Sheer
waste... That's the trouble with our society... Waste...
waste... too much waste... look around you... everywhere...
all you can see is waste... waste... everything's wasting...
wasting away... (*He starts to pace the room.*) Everywhere you
look, waste... and muck. (*He lifts up the kettle.*) Look, muck...
(*He slams it down and picks up the pot.*) More muck... waste
and muck... (*He slams that down and goes to the sink.*) More
muck... everywhere... is full of muck. Muck. Someone
else's muck... It's all waste... all waste I tell
you. Everything's going to waste!!

MARTIN: Well no one wants muck, do they?

RYDER: It wasn't always muck. It wasn't muck when it
started, was it?... (*He picks up the pot and shows it to MARTIN.*)
Was that muck... was that always muck? Did the people
that cooked that... did they cook muck...? Is that what
they cooked... muck?

MARTIN: They were foreigners... They were foreigners had
this room.

RYDER: Did it start out as muck... was it muck when it
started?

MARTIN: That's them foreigners done that. That's their
muck. They left that muck there... (*He slams the pot down.*)

RYDER: Muck!!! The country's full of it. Everywhere you
go... the stench of muck in your nostrils.

MARTIN: It's them foreigners that done that I tell you...
That's their muck... foreign muck that is.

RYDER: Foreigners! We're all foreigners.

MARTIN: I'm not a foreigner.

RYDER: Everyone's a foreigner. None of us belong here.

MARTIN: Eh... Here... listen... I'm not a foreigner.

RYDER: (*Turning to him.*) You're muck! Did you start out as muck! Was you muck when you started?

MARTIN: Eh?

RYDER: Why didn't you jump under that train this morning? You should have done, you know... You should have jumped under it.

MARTIN: Eh... what... Why should I go and jump under trains?

RYDER: You were going to jump under one this morning. You said you were.

MARTIN: Eh... Well, I... Yer, well... Look I don't want to jump under no trains if I don't want to... What do you think I am? Eh... an old twat... or something... go and jump under trains... just to please you.

RYDER: You were lying. You had no intention of jumping under any trains. It was a lie. A big act... trying to get sympathy... That's what you were after... that's about the size of what you were after. I'm on your game... You don't fool me. You were expecting someone to rush out and stop you... put half a crown in your hand and stop you. It was no soap... was it... It was no soap... didn't wash... did it? No one's bothered. Who's bothered... You won't see no headlines. Old Winston Churchill... he dies in bed... natural causes... Headlines... Headlines all over the world... But a bit of muck... chucks himself under a train... who's bothered... The porters... they got to sweep it up... they're bothered perhaps... no one else. What's it matter... what's it matter, they say... Only a bit of old muck.

MARTIN: Yer... I know... I know. That's it... That's it. What
you were saying... that's it... I know... I stood there...
I told 'em. I stood there and told 'em... I'm going to be
under it I said. I stood there and told 'em... I told 'em
straight... I'm fed up I said, I'm fed up with it all. No
food I ain't had, no breakfast, I might as well be dead
I said... I might as well be dead. And I'm going to end
it I said... I said to 'em... I said I'm going to chuck
myself under the next train that comes in... the next
train I said... and not one of them... comes forward to
stop me... not one of 'em tried to stop me. I could have
gone and done for all they'd care. If I was potty enough
I could have chucked meself under that train. Makes you
sick, don' it... People... stand and watch you do away with
yourself and not one of 'em... not one of 'em'd lift a hand
to stop you. All they'd do... sprinkle a bit of sawdust on
you... and start a moan going 'cos the trains were late.
(*He sits on the bed*.) Not one of them stinking rotten sods
would have bothered... I could have killed myself there
this morning, and not one of them stinking rotten sods
would have bothered. Not one of 'em. You saw it didn't
you... You saw it... Not one of 'em rushed forward to stop
me. I could have killed meself down there. Makes you
sick don' it. Eh? Makes you wanna puke don' it... They're
muck... That's all they are, muck. You're right... It's what
they are... muck.

RYDER: You ought to go and see that psychologist. He'd
straighten you out. I reckon he'd straighten you out
alright. He's a good man. He'd fix you up well.

MARTIN: I'm not a loony... I'm not one of those bleeding
Lulus.

RYDER: It's a bad habit you've got. This suicide thing...
It's a bad habit you've got there. You want to get that
cured.

MARTIN: Cured? I ain't got no suicide habit, mate. That's no habit... all that down there on that platform... That ain't no suicide habit. You've got the wrong end of the stick there, mate... you've got it the wrong way round. You saw me on a bad day... that's the gist of that. Look... listen... You see me on a good day... You see me down there on that platform on a good day... I get about four half crowns doing that little bit. There's nothing lulu about all that.

RYDER: How long have you been doing that?

MARTIN: About three and a half years on an' off... You can't work it too often like... You have to go a bit easy on it. I mean there ain't many stations... if you get my meaning... unless you want to get involved in a lot of fares... travelling expenses like... travelling around. Them porters soon twig you... get down there too often... they soon twig you... an' it's nick... if you ain't careful... my age... can't afford no nick... too much porridge'd do for me. I ain't getting any younger. Them toerags soon get on to you. No, you seen me on a bad day... that's the gist of that. Tell you the time... Tell you the time you want to see me work that little bit. Xmas... Xmas Eve... When they got all their presents... and a few drinks see, that's the time you want to see me work that bit. I've made thirty bob... Xmas Eve... before now... doing that little bit... drinks... I've had drinks off 'em too. One year... Yer... one year... It was one year... one year it was... I got invited home. (*Chuckles.*) Parson it was... proper upset he was... about my condition... took me home he did. His wife didn't like the idea. She wasn't very pleased about it at all... I had a rotten Xmas... What with him and her – and all that bleeding religion. 'Bout the worst one I've ever had... All that religion. I don't go for that stuff... What I always say... I always say... if the Lord... God I mean... if he...

RYDER: You talk too much.

MARTIN: Eh?

RYDER: That's your trouble you know... You go on...

MARTIN: What?

RYDER: That's what's wrong with you. You don't give yourself a rest. No one gets a chance with you.

MARTIN: Talk? Too much? Who me?

RYDER: Yes. Haven't you ever noticed? You get started. You start rabbiting... and it seems like you can't stop... you don't know where to end. No one ever told you that before?

MARTIN: No... I ain't ever heard that before. No one's ever told me that... I've met a lot of people. I've known a lot of people in my time... No one's ever said that though.

RYDER: Your one drawback... It's your one drawback...

Pause.

RYDER: What do you think of this room?

MARTIN: This room?

RYDER: Yes... you want to learn to listen. People prefer listeners... They like listeners.

MARTIN: Yes... I suppose.

Pause.

RYDER: (*Looking around.*) You could do things with this room. Big things... don't you think? A lot of things you could do. (*He walks round and MARTIN watches him.*) I've got a chair coming. It'll be a lot better when I get the chair.

MARTIN: (*Walks round with him.*) It's a good room.

RYDER: Yes. That's what I've been thinking. I need a place. I've got to settle. This could be ideal.

MARTIN: That's what I want.

RYDER: What?

MARTIN: A room... a room like this...

RYDER: Yes. It needs things doing... few improvements...

MARTIN: You could do 'em though... You could do 'em in
this room... There's something here to work on.

RYDER: I've got a lampshade coming...

MARTIN: (*Looks up at bulb.*) There's not one here... not now...
you haven't got one.

RYDER: It's coming... I've got one coming...

   Pause.

MARTIN: That's funny that is. That's very funny.

RYDER: What?

MARTIN: I've never been told that before... Not never...

RYDER: What?

MARTIN: What you said... I talk too much.

RYDER: You do?

MARTIN: Yes.

RYDER: I haven't noticed.

MARTIN: You said... The dogs can be heard barking again.

   They both listen.

MARTIN: Them dogs... Them bleeding dogs!!

RYDER: We ought to get up a petition about them.
A petition... that's what they need. We ought to get
one up.

MARTIN: Who'd sign it?

RYDER: Me and you... We'd sign it.

MARTIN: What about Ellis, say he found out?

RYDER: Make it a round robin.

A door shuts and the dogs stop.

RYDER: They're not supposed to have dogs... like that... not in a place like this... It's not a kennels is it?

MARTIN: No... It's not a kennels.

Pause. RYDER walks around the room again... looking.

RYDER: I've got to think about this. There's things I want to do about this... this room... I want to think about it... Do you want a job?

MARTIN: A job?

RYDER: I'm looking for staff. I'm in the market for staff you see. Good staff. I don't want any old rubbish. No union men. Nothing like that.

MARTIN: What... Work you mean?

RYDER: You'd have to work... be a good job... pension scheme, bonus scheme, superannuation, prospects, sickness scheme, advancement... nothing like that.

MARTIN: I'd have to think about it. Needs thought... you see... taking a job... I wouldn't want to rush into anything.

RYDER: Choosey eh?

MARTIN: You've got to be... It's got to be considered. There's a lot of jobs... blind alleys a lot of 'em... You get nowhere like that... I've worked on me own you see... my own boss, always have been.

RYDER: That's the sort of men I'm looking for. Men with character... make decisions.

MARTIN: How many men are you thinking about? What do you need... I mean, how many?

RYDER: Depends... I'm thinking of enlarging you see... spreading out... That's what I'm here for... widen me net. That's why I left Manchester... Too small... You've got to be able to move around. You've got to be big... It's no good being small... get you nowhere.

MARTIN: What you in?

RYDER: How do you mean?

MARTIN: Your business... What do you do?

RYDER: I used to be a surgeon... brain surgeon.

MARTIN: Get away...

RYDER: Yes... In Manchester... Best one they had in Manchester. I worked in a big hospital there... I can't remember the name of it... big place though... very modern... full of equipment it was... good stuff... first rate stuff. They thought a lot of me up there... In Manchester... Didn't want me to leave.

MARTIN: No... I suppose they wouldn't.

RYDER: Good men are hard to find.

MARTIN: I know... You can't get em.

RYDER: Perhaps you could help me...

MARTIN: Help you?

RYDER: If you hear of anyone... you know... anyone wants any brain surgery done... Let me now... put in a word for me. I do a good job.

MARTIN: Yes... I will. If I hear of anything... I'll mention you.

RYDER: You won't forget.

MARTIN: No.

RYDER: Here's my card... (*He brings out a card and hands it to MARTIN. MARTIN takes it and reads it.*)

MARTIN: Yes... er... (*He goes to put it in his pocket.*)

RYDER: Don't take that... It's the only one I've got.

MARTIN: Oh... I see. (*He hands it back.*)

RYDER: I couldn't get any more printed. This chap that did it... you see, he's moved... I don't know where to contact him.

Pause.

MARTIN: (*Listens.*) What's that... footsteps. It's Sophia... I got to go. (*He makes for the door. Opens it and goes out furtively and in a great hurry.*)

After a few seconds SOPHIA enters carrying a chair and a lampshade. Also a newspaper.

SOPHIA: Ellis was very pleased.

RYDER: Eh?

SOPHIA: About you staying. He likes people who stay. (*She puts the chair down and puts the lampshade on it.*) They'll have to go on an inventory.

RYDER: You mean... sign for them?

SOPHIA: Yes... You'll have to sign for them.

RYDER: (*Half picks up the lampshade.*) I've got to take the responsibility... I've got to be responsible... you mean?

SOPHIA: Yes.

RYDER drops the lampshade back on the seat as though it had suddenly become hot.

RYDER: I don't know... I don't know about that... I'll have to think about that.

SOPHIA: You've got to accept responsibilities... this room...
you see, it's all got to be signed for.

RYDER: Huh. I didn't know that. You didn't say that.

SOPHIA: It's normal procedure... It's always done.

RYDER: I wasn't given to understand that. I wasn't
informed. I haven't been informed you know...
about that...

SOPHIA: It's only a piece of paper... You've just got to sign
it that's all... It won't take you a minute. (*She shows him
scrap of paper.*)

RYDER: (*Looks hunted... backs away slightly.*) I... don't know...
I... I don't know about that...

SOPHIA: It's just your signature... that's all we want...
just your signature.

RYDER: I... I haven't got a pencil. (*Brightens.*) I haven't got
a pencil. You can't sign without a pencil it's impossible.

SOPHIA: I've got a pen. (*She hands him a pen. Biro type.*)

RYDER: (*Looks at it without taking it.*) No... it's a biro.

SOPHIA: Ball point.

RYDER: You can't use those... not for signatures. The banks
won't accept them. You'll have to get a pencil... (*He makes
a decision.*) I won't sign without a pencil.

Pause. She looks at him.

RYDER: It's a nice chair... I like the chair.

SOPHIA: What about the lampshade?

RYDER: I wanted one with beer labels... You can't get one
with beer labels?

SOPHIA: I'll see Ellis... You'd have to sign.

RYDER: (*Eagerly.*) I'd sign for that... Yes I like them. I'd sign for one of those...

SOPHIA: I brought the paper up... thought you might like to have a read...

RYDER: (*Takes it.*) Oh yes... today's is it?

SOPHIA: Just come out... we get 'em fresh here. The boy brings 'em. We got an arrangement... mornings and evenings everyday...

RYDER: Hm... I like reading the papers... you get a lot of news in them...

SOPHIA: There's a lot of news in it today... quite a lot...

Pause while RYDER reads the paper.

SOPHIA: I see they've been writing to each other again.

RYDER: Eh?

SOPHIA: Those two... they been writing some more letters to each other.

RYDER: Who?

SOPHIA: Mr MacMillan and that Kruschev fellow.

Pause.

SOPHIA: Do you think they'll drop it?

RYDER: Eh?

SOPHIA: That bomb... do you think they'll drop it?

RYDER: (*Still scanning the paper.*) Oh...

SOPHIA: Ellis is worried... He doesn't know what to do about his dogs... I mean if they drop it... if they drop it I mean...

Pause.

SOPHIA: I see that bloke has arrived down here.

RYDER: Who?

SOPHIA: That bloke... that one from Manchester... the one that's been killing all them girls... He must have arrived last night I reckon... He's done one in this morning... they've found her murdered... dead she was. No handbag... he's taken the handbag again.

Pause.

SOPHIA: I wonder why he always takes their handbags?

Pause.

SOPHIA: Sex...

Pause.

SOPHIA: Do you reckon it's sex?

RYDER: What?

SOPHIA: Them handbags... taking their handbags... after he's killed them... Do you reckon it might be sex?

Pause.

SOPHIA: I reckon it is... I reckon it's sex...

Pause.

SOPHIA: That or money.

RYDER: (*Hands her back the paper.*) I don't want to read this... I don't like reading papers... Not this sort... I like the Times... The Financial Times... I'm a business man... I can't afford to read those sorts of papers... I'm in business.

SOPHIA: Shall I tell Ellis?

RYDER: Yes... Tell him. Go down and tell him... I want a posher sort of paper... I'm not a working man... Go and tell him... He ought to know how I feel about these sort of things. He's got to know me... If I'm going to live here... he's got to get to know me. Go and tell him.

SOPHIA picks up the lampshade.

SOPHIA: And you want one with beer labels?

RYDER: Yes. They're a better class of thing... much better than that.

SOPHIA goes out. The door has hardly closed when MARTIN creeps in.

MARTIN: She's brought my chair in here... I was watching... I was watching round the corner... I saw her. She's been in my room and brought my chair in here.

RYDER: That's my chair...

MARTIN: It's out of my room.

RYDER: It's on my inventory.

MARTIN: I see their game... That's that bleeding Ellis... He's trying to get at me... taking my chair... He knows that's my chair. That's what he's done. He's told her to take it...

RYDER: I've got to sign for that.

MARTIN: The bastards. They're bastards the pair of 'em... That's because I've paid no rent... I know what it is... that's what upset 'em. I wouldn't stop here... If I had somewhere else... I wouldn't stop here.

RYDER: You under contract?

MARTIN: Eh?

RYDER: They got you under contract?

MARTIN: No... they won't have me. Bleeding bastards...
. Rent mad... That's what they are... bleeding rent mad.
I'll get 'em. I'll get down there one night... If I get a bit
of drink in me... I'll knife that Ellis. They ain't seen me
with a bit of drink in me... You'll see... He'll get a knife.
He'll get a bleeding knife he will. (*He sits down in the chair,
mumbling to himself... furious.*) I see it. They're supposed to
make me comfortable they are... It's all clear... It's
coming clear now. If I want to sit on my own chair... I've
got to come in here... in a foreign room... sit in me own
chair. 'Cos I ain't got no rent... that's the bottom of it...
that's the root... that's where it is...

He is half mumbling all this... more to himself.

RYDER sits on the bed, deep in thought.

RYDER: (*Half to himself.*) They're trying to get me under
contract. It's all this signing... they want me to keep
signing things.

Pause. They are both occupied with their own thoughts.

RYDER: Do you still want this job?

MARTIN: I ain't thought... I've not had time to think
about it.

RYDER: You'd have to pass some tests... aptitude tests...
psychological tests... nothing hard. I can do them... most
people can do them... and a few entrance exams. Mostly
civil service stuff... I've got the papers... Have you had a
good education?

MARTIN: Eh? Who me?

RYDER: I did... I went to a good school... Very good
school... elementary... but very good.

MARTIN: Same as me.

RYDER: Eh?

MARTIN: I went there.

RYDER: Where?

MARTIN: Elementary...

RYDER: I think you'd do, you know. I think you might be alright... You could come for an interview I suppose.

MARTIN: Interview?

RYDER: For the job... You'd have to have an interview... I could fit you in tomorrow morning... say about nine o'clock... Yes that'd be the best I think... tomorrow at nine... (*He gets up, picks up his case and puts it on the bed, just near where MARTIN is sitting.*) I suppose you've got references... You'll need those. (*He opens the case. MARTIN looks in it.*)

MARTIN: What's them?

RYDER: Handbags... secondhand... handbags...

MARTIN: Secondhand... handbags... what for... what are they for?

RYDER: I sell them. That's my business... I told you I'm in business...

Scene Two

RYDER's room, about half an hour later. RYDER in his underpants is fixing the last of six new bolts on his door... as he works... a door opens downstairs and the dogs start to bark. He listens to them... and then he carries on with his work. He finishes the bolt, and then shoots all six new bolts home and tries the door. The door won't budge, being held firmly by the bolts, and he appears satisfied with his work. He puts on his suit, unbolts the door and goes out into the dark and shadowy hallway. He closes the door of his room, and stands looking at it.

RYDER: There should be a key. I should have a key to this... (*He stands there looking round, very uncertain.*) There ought to be a key... No good having a room without a key...

He reaches a decision and after one more apprehensive look round the hallway he hurries downstairs. MARTIN's door opens and MARTIN pops his head out. He looks after RYDER... very still, waiting. The front door downstairs slams shut. MARTIN gives a little smile and creeps furtively out of his room and hurries over to RYDER's room and goes in. He tries to open the two suitcases but they are locked. He rummages round the room, looks in the cupboard which is empty, opens the gas open and finds a sandwich in there. He starts to scoff it. He hears a noise outside and stiffens, listening. RYDER appears at the top of the stairs and walks towards his room. MARTIN hears him and hides in the cupboard. RYDER enters his room and shoots home all the bolts. He takes his suit off and puts it on the hanger. He fixes the hanger to the top of the cupboard. He then opens one of the suitcases and takes out a razor and strap and proceeds to sharpen the razor. When it is sharpened to his satisfaction he goes over to the line of pin-ups and talks to the picture at the end of the line.

RYDER: (*Spits at it at first.*) You dirty little wretch. You filthy little slut. (*He tears the picture off the wall, puts it on the table and viciously cuts it up with the razor. He works savagely and maniacally, muttering all the time.*) You dirty... dirty... filthy little stripper you... You poncing little prostitute... Money grabbing little beast. (*He finishes his work and goes back to the other pictures. He looks at the one next in line and spits at that too.*) It's your turn tomorrow my beauty... I'll give you smile. (*He spits on it again.*) You're getting the same as she got tomorrow... that'll take the smile off your face. You dirty naked little swine.

During this the door of the cupboard opens slightly, and shuts again quickly and quietly. RYDER takes control of himself and then slowly looks up to the picture of the Queen.

RYDER: (*He speaks as though praying.*) Please forgive me for I have sinned. But... (*He looks at the pin-ups again and almost goes off once more.*) But these indecent creatures are not fit to be your subjects. I'll do away with them all. I'll make your land a clean and decent place to live in...

He shuts the razor and puts it back in the suitcase with the strap... He then takes off his vest and puts his pyjama coat on... it is long and covers his knees. He takes his pants off from under it and puts the pyjama trousers on. He opens the suitcase again and takes out a gramophone... he puts it on the table. He then takes out a record and rubbing it lovingly with the sleeve of his pyjama coat for a few seconds... perhaps to get any dust off it... puts it on the gramophone and plays it. There is a loud roll of timps from the record as a prelude to a heavily orchestrated rendering of God Save the Queen. *As the record hits the first note of* God Save the Queen, *RYDER springs to attention, facing the picture of the Queen, brings up his hands in a smart salute, and holding the saluting position as the record plays...*

ACT TWO

Scene One

RYDER's room. The next morning. RYDER is up, and wearing his pants and vest, is just finishing putting six more new bolts on his door. He finishes his work, shoots all the bolts home again, and tries the door. It appears fastened to his satisfaction. He puts his suit on, unfastens the bolts and goes out. He stands outside the door looking at it. He is in a very unsettled state of mind about the door, perturbed because there is no key on the outside. He goes down the stairs... as soon as he is gone, MARTIN creeps out of the cupboard and hurries out of the room to his own room. RYDER comes back, followed by SOPHIA. They go to RYDER's door.

RYDER: I've got to have a key for this door you see... I can't leave it unlocked like this. It's no good to me like that.

SOPHIA: (*Looks at door, thinking.*) Hm. Well, the thing is you see... Hm... You want it locked?

RYDER: Yes. I can't leave it like that.

SOPHIA: (*Looks at the door.*) Hm... The thing is you see... Ellis doesn't like these rooms locked... that's the snag. He likes to be able to get in and out of them you see.

RYDER: Hm. That's all very well. That's what he wants... that's not what I want... I mean this is my room... isn't it? It's been let to me this room hasn't it?

SOPHIA: Yes... and you want to lock it?

RYDER: Well of course. I mean I don't want Ellis... or anyone else for that matter... in and out of here all day long. I mean this is my place... I mean this is where I live. That's the way I want to keep it... I mean I've got my privacy to think of you see.

SOPHIA: Hm. I see your point... But he wouldn't bother you. I mean if that's all you're worried about, he wouldn't do that... He'd leave you to be private.

RYDER: Well that's all I want. But if he's going to be in and out all day... I mean you can't call that private... That's not being private is it... That's not privacy.

SOPHIA: That's what I'm saying... He wouldn't do that... He wouldn't come in while you were there... He'll only pop in while you were out... I mean you wouldn't even see him.

RYDER: That's fine. That's marvellous isn't it? I mean that's not the sort of room I wanted. You didn't mention that in your letter. When I booked this room you didn't say anything about that... About him popping in and out.

While they are talking MARTIN pops his head round the door listening.

SOPHIA: Well, he likes to check on the fittings you see – I mean he likes to know what's going on.

RYDER hears MARTIN, who has nipped back behind his door.

RYDER: (*Putting his finger to his mouth.*) Sssh...

He creeps along to MARTIN's door and stands listening with his ear pressed to the door... then he bends down and puts his eye to the keyhole... He gets up and comes back to SOPHIA.

RYDER: You see, that's the sort of thing... that's what you've got to be on the watch for. Spying... that's the second time I've caught him. That's why I want a key. I can't go out and leave my door unlocked with him over there... I've got a lot of valuable stuff in that room. I've got some very valuable properties in there. I carry a lot of stock in my business and it's all in there... I mean anyone

134

like him gets his hands on that... That's the sort of
chance he'd be looking for... someone like him. That's
what all the spying's for... that's the way they work.

SOPHIA: Well you could always tell if he's been in there.

RYDER: Tell?

SOPHIA: I mean if he takes anything... I mean you'd soon
know... You'd easy find out.

RYDER: Yes. You've got to have proof though. You need
proof.

SOPHIA: You wouldn't need much proof against him.
I mean it's not as though he was honest. If he was an
honest person... I mean you've got to have a lot of proof
against honest persons... But someone like him... I mean
you wouldn't need no proof at all hardly.

RYDER: Yes well that's alright you see... but I wouldn't want
to get no police involved, that's the trouble. I don't deal
with them. You know... nothing against them... They've
got their ways... It's a personal thing... That's all... that's
all it is.

Pause.

RYDER: You don't get them round here do you?

SOPHIA: Who?

RYDER: The police... They don't come poking their noses
round here, do they?

SOPHIA: No not as a rule. We've got them coming though.
They're coming round here... You could tell them then...
if he's taken anything. They could have him then... save
'em coming round special like...

RYDER: Are they coming in here?

SOPHIA: What – the police?

RYDER: Yes... they coming in here?

SOPHIA: Yes... so they said... They came round this
morning... said they'd be coming. A young chap it was...
and an older fellow. Good looking the young chap was...
very polite... nice spoken too. They want all the names
they said.

RYDER: Names... what names?

SOPHIA: Everyone's... It's about the murders... you know
all these young girls that keep getting killed. They want
to talk to us about it... There was one done in last night.
Just up the road... I told 'em... I said I reckon it's sex...
that's what's behind it... That's why he takes the
handbags. Don't you think so?

RYDER: Did you give 'em my name?

SOPHIA: I didn't give him any names yet. They're coming
back you see. That's when they want the names... when
they come back. That's what they're coming back for
you see... for the names.

RYDER: I'd rather you didn't give them my name actually...
You see I'd prefer it if you didn't mention me at all...
You see when they come back... the best thing you could
do is not mention me. That's the easiest way... don't give
them my name. They don't know I'm here. They're got
no record.

SOPHIA: Yes, but it's the names they want... that's what
they're coming back for... They want all the names...
everyone's. That's what they come round to ask for.

RYDER: They don't want my name though... They didn't
ask for my name did they? I mean it's simple isn't it...
I'm not the murderer... what would they want my name
for? I mean if you give 'em my name it's just wasting
their time... They don't want to talk to me. It's the
murderer they want to talk to...

SOPHIA: No... They want to talk to all of us. Everyone down the street. They're going to talk to everyone. That's what they're coming round for...

RYDER: (*Looks round furtively, puts his fingers to his lips.*) Sssh... (*He opens his door and beckons her in.*) Come in here...

SOPHIA follows him into his room. He shoots all the bolts home.

SOPHIA: (*Watches him.*) What are you doing that for?

RYDER: We don't want to be disturbed... I've got something important to tell you. You don't know this... but I'm from Scotland Yard.

SOPHIA: You?

RYDER: I'm one of the big heads up there. You didn't know that did you? You didn't know I was the head of Scotland Yard did you?

SOPHIA: What? Eh?... Get away...

RYDER: You wouldn't think it... would you?.. To look at me... You wouldn't think I was the head of Scotland Yard would you? Go on, own up... You wouldn't... would you?

SOPHIA: No...

RYDER: That's why they picked me... Cos' I didn't look like it... that's the way they work up there. Everything has to be kept secret you see. No-one's allowed to know who I am. Not even the police.

SOPHIA: Eh?

RYDER: That's why you mustn't tell them I'm here. If they found out I was here they'd be in trouble. It'd spoil everything... There'd be a few heads would roll then... I can tell you... You don't want to end up in prison do you?

SOPHIA: Who me? I haven't done anything.

RYDER: If you interfere with the police in the execution of their duty... I suppose you know the law don't you?

SOPHIA: Well er...

RYDER: I better warn you first... that anything you say may be taken down and used in evidence against you... or *prima facie*... as the case may be. So watch out... you're dealing with tricky people now. What's your name?

SOPHIA: Sophia Wheeling.

RYDER: Is that your real name? I don't want any false names you know... Watch it... you're dealing with the police now... The law's fair in this country... but just get in its way mate... and you'll get a clout over the nut.

SOPHIA: Sophia Wheeling.

RYDER: I see, still sticking to that name are you? Alright. It's up to you. Please yourself. But don't say you haven't been warned.

SOPHIA: Who do you think you are... You can't talk to me like that. (*She turns to the door.*) Unbolt this door.

RYDER: Look mate, watch out. You're dealing with the wrong sort of people now. I could give you six months and a belt over the head for less than that... You can't sod the bleeding police about you know... You don't think we're here to be pissed around with do you? Now sit down.

SOPHIA: No... I want to go... Let me out.

RYDER: Yes... that's what they all say. (*He pushes her onto the bed.*) Listen ma-am... I want the fact ma-am... just the facts ma-am... that's all ma-am... just the facts. Where were you on the fourteenth ma-am... on the fourteenth ma-am... where were you then?

SOPHIA: (*Jumps up.*) Oh don't be silly... I'm...

RYDER: (*Hurls her back savagely onto the bed.*) It's not me that's being silly... it's you that's being bloody silly... you're the bleeding silly one. (*He grabs the cut-throat razor out of the case and brandishes it.*) See this... see this... Now watch it. I've got the power to use this. I'm not in Scotland Yard for nothing you know. They taught us how to use these in the police college, mate. I've been trained... In my hands this could be a deadly weapon... I'm no bleeding barber... I ain't got this because I'm a barber you know...

She backs round the bed and he creeps round after her, brandishing the razor. There is knock at the door.

RYDER: (*Puts his finger to his mouth. To SOPHIA.*) ... Sssh. Come in...

MARTIN: Eh... I can't get the door open.

RYDER: I think it must have stuck... Come back when it's not stuck. (*He winks at SOPHIA.*)

MARTIN: Eh?

RYDER: It's the warm weather... It makes the door swell... Expands it... that's why it's stuck. You'll have to wait until it contracts.

MARTIN: Eh? What's going on in there?

RYDER: Mind your own business you nosey old bugger... Sod off.

While he is talking, RYDER takes a long, thin cane out of his case and creeps towards the door... sidling along the wall... when he is alongside the door, he poises the cane and jabs it hard through the keyhole. There is a terrific yell from outside and MARTIN who has been apparent in shadow peering through the keyhole, leaps up holding his eye in agony, and runs to his room.

RYDER: (*Winks at SOPHIA again.*) Another little police trick. That ought to keep his minces out of my keyhole... handy for that these things are you know... Nice and thin you see. (*Shows her the cane.*) Go through the hole nicely. (*Pokes in keyhole again.*) I've got hundreds of 'em. (*He goes to case and takes out a huge pile of thin canes. He lets them fall onto the table.*) Lovely aren't they? I used to be a school teacher... that's why I've got all of them... You need them in a school... hundreds of them you need... (*He swishes one savagely.*) They sting you know... You try it...

He makes a slash at SOPHIA with the cane and catches her across the back. She yells with pain.

RYDER: Hurt don't they? Alright fair's fair... You can hit me with one now... go on.

SOPHIA: No... Let me go. Let me go.

RYDER: No fair's fair... You hit me with one... come on... I don't mind...

She backs away from him around the table and he follows her trying to persuade her to take the cane.

RYDER: Come on, I don't mind... I deserve it... I've been naughty. Here you are... I can't be fairer than that.

SOPHIA: Open the door – I want to leave.

RYDER: Don't be silly... No one's going to hurt you... It's alright... I'm not going to hurt you.

She backs away from him.

SOPHIA: If you touch me I'll scream... Ellis'll come up here then. He'll get the police... You'd better let me out, otherwise you'll be sorry.

RYDER: You're not very friendly are you... I thought you were the friendly type when I first met you... I had you all wrong didn't I?

SOPHIA: Friendly? I wouldn't be friendly with you... Not your sort.

RYDER: What's wrong with my sort? Eh? What's wrong with my sort then?

SOPHIA: You know what's wrong... There's something wrong with you alright.

RYDER: I suppose there's nothing wrong with you? You're perfect I suppose. I suppose you're perfect... (*Puts the cane down and starts to finger the razor.*)

They are going round and the table... she backing away and RYDER following her.

SOPHIA: Don't you come near me... Don't you touch me with that.

RYDER: (*Looks at razor and smiles.*) You're frightened of this aren't you? You're scared stiff of it... aren't you? Go on, own up... you don't like it do you? (*He fingers it again.*) Very good for shaving these are you know... How would you like me to give you a shave... Eh? Shave your head... Shave all that mangy old hair off, eh? Improve your looks that would you know.

He suddenly changes direction and darts round the other side of the table after her. She turns and runs in the other direction to avoid him, but he is too quick and grabs her. He holds her by the hair.

RYDER: Now keep quiet... One shout out of you and... (*He brandishes the razor in her face. He forces her into a chair.*) Sit down...

MARTIN's door opens and MARTIN, still holding his eye, runs out. He pauses at RYDER's door and bangs on it.

MARTIN: You bastard... I'll get you for this... You won't take liberties with me, mate... You'll pay for this... you see.

He runs to stairs and goes down them.

141

RYDER: What do you let him stay here for? You ought to get rid of him... You'll never run a decent house like that... with undesirables like him in it They get the place a bad name... You'll find all your decent people leaving. (*He is still holding her by the hair.*) Nice hair you've got, haven't you? Been dyed hasn't it... The old roots are coming through black now. (*He pulls her head back and looks at her.*) You're not a bad looking girl really are you... sort of girl who could drive a man mad you are. Anyone ever told you you were good looking... Not lately. Not recently I shouldn't think. I bet you were a bit of a beauty when you were young, though. Still you're not old now are you? I bet you're not a day over fifty...

SOPHIA: Don't you start anything with me.

RYDER: Start anything? Who's starting anything... You come in my room... What do you expect, eh? You come in my room... let me bolt the door so we wouldn't be disturbed... What do you expect? You must expect me to start something...

SOPHIA: Let go of my hair... You're hurting me...

She tries to pull his hands away.

RYDER: Stop it... Stop it I say... Ooooh... you'll get it in a minute.

SOPHIA: (*Stops struggling, terrified.*) Don't you touch me... you touch me... there'll be trouble. You'll be in trouble, I tell you.

RYDER: So, I'll be in trouble will I... so you're going to make trouble for me are you? (*He puts the razor up close to her throat.*)

SOPHIA: No... I won't make any trouble... I won't... I won't make any.

RYDER: I know you won't... I know you won't make any trouble. I mean how could you? 'Cos... you know what I'm

going to do? We're going to have a bit of fun with you,
me beauty... We're going to have some fun... right now...

*He makes a movement to her with the razor. The lights blackout and
SOPHIA screams long and shrill and the screams seem to end
strangled in her throat.*

Curtains descends.

Scene Two

*MARTIN's room. Very late that night... It is a room very much like
RYDER's but a lot smaller. It contains no furniture at all, expect a
broken sink. There is a window in one wall with a sack covering the
bottom half. And on the floor a bed has been made up... in this lies
MARTIN fast asleep. After a few seconds the sack covering the bottom
half of the window is pushed aside and RYDER climbs in... He
moves very stealthily. Once in the room he brings out his razor and
creeps towards where MARTIN lies asleep... He bends over him and
putting the razor to his throat, shakes him slightly to wake him up.
MARTIN wakes with a start. Very conscious of the razor at his
throat. Bring the lights up very slowly to reveal the scene... and to
show huge bandage round MARTIN's head and eye...*

RYDER: (*Puts his fingers to his lips.*) Sssh... don't make any
noise... I just popped in. I noticed you'd been avoiding
me lately... so I thought I'd just pop in... see what was the
matter... have it out like. You're holding a grudge aren't
you... against me... Come on own up. Something's upset
you hasn't it? Eh? Come on, what have I done?

MARTIN: Eh? What you done? Look at... (*He points to
his eye.*) My eye... look... I 'ad to go to Moorfields...
that's where I've been with that... that eye. It's almost
no good.

RYDER: Ah, so that's what it is. I knew there was something
you was holding against me... I knew you had something
up your snout... I'm sensitive. I can sense things... I can
always tell when there's a bit of feeling going on.

MARTIN: Eh? Feeling... Bit of feeling you say... Look at that eye... Look at it. Look what you've done... jabbing it like that. It's almost no good that eye... I almost lost it... The bloke down at Moorfields... that doctor... He said I almost lost it...

RYDER: Alright so I hurt your eye... I'm sorry... I've said I'm sorry. Blimey, we can still be friends can't we? It's no good getting like that about it... going against your friends. You've got to learn to take a bit of fun you know. It was only a bit of larking... that's all it was... Christ... You're not a kid are you... go round sulking over a little joke.

MARTIN: You might think it was just a joke... I almost lost an eye... that eye's almost no good.

RYDER: Well I mean... if you're going to be nosey. Let's face it, you were poking your nose in weren't you?

MARTIN: No... eh? I was only having a look... I thought I heard voices in there. That's why... I thought I heard voices... so I had a look. That's all I done... I wasn't nosing. I wasn't doing that.

RYDER: Voices? What voices?

MARTIN: In your room. There was someone in there talking. Shouting they were.

RYDER: In my room? No you've got the wrong end of the stick there, mate... You've got it all wrong there mate... There's been no one in my room...

MARTIN: Eh? But I heard 'em. It was you and Sophie. I heard 'em...

RYDER: Sophie... You mean her downstairs? No... She's not been in my room... I haven't seen her...

MARTIN: That's what it sounded like... It sounded like her.

RYDER: No, she's not been in my room. Well she did come in. Started having a go at me... You know, put her arms round me and all that sort of stuff... wanted me to start mucking about with her... But I wasn't having any. Wouldn't leave me alone she wouldn't... Had her hands everywhere... So I told her to go that's all. I had to chuck her out in the end... crying she was...

MARTIN: Well when I looked in you was... (*Stops, thinks better of it.*)

RYDER: What?

MARTIN: Eh?

RYDER: I said what? When you looked in I was what?

MARTIN: Oh... nothing... nothing.

RYDER: No I wouldn't have her in my room... Not her... that ugly moo... She sleeps with that bloody Indian downstairs... that's her trouble. I wouldn't have her in my room.

Pause.

RYDER: What time was it?

MARTIN: What?

RYDER: When you reckon you heard her... in my room.

MARTIN: When you done that eye... this morning... when you done my eye. That's what I was looking in for... I thought perhaps she might be in there nicking something. She's a thief you know... that one... She's a bloody thief. She's always in here mooching around... That's why I looked in... I thought – We're friends like –

RYDER: Don't worry about her... She won't be in anymore...

MARTIN: Eh? Why? Why's that then?

145

RYDER: She's gone away...

MARTIN: Gone away? She ain't told Ellis. It was Ellis asked me if I'd seen her.

RYDER: She never told him. She didn't want him to know. She's gone up to Manchester... She don't want him to know... so he won't follow her... She wants it kept a secret.

MARTIN: She told you that?

RYDER: Yes. She said not to tell anyone. She's got her family up there... She wants to see them.

MARTIN: Her family live in Ireland.

RYDER: They've moved to Manchester... they've gone to meet her. (*He looks round.*) Nice room you've got here.

MARTIN: Yer... it does me. Not what I want... but it does alright.

The bed, a made-up one, comprises a mattress in a wooden frame, slung across two boxes. RYDER now starts to idly cut at it with the razor.

RYDER: I've been thinking of taking another room.

MARTIN: Yer?

RYDER: Mine's not what I want you see. Do you like circular rooms?

MARTIN: Circular? What... you mean round?

RYDER: Yes... Sort of like a lighthouse... all round... you know... I had a dream about a room like that you know... very round sort it was you know... sort of... very round. This landlord he was trying to sell me it... this room. He wanted two hundred quid for it... I said No... I said I'll give you eight hundred for it... not a penny less. He said he wouldn't sell it for that much... And then he started playing with my peter... Committing the old fellatio on me... I said you can pack that in, I said... If you expect me to buy this room you can turn that in... I don't like people playing with my peter... I asked him to let go... but he wouldn't... I knew he wouldn't... He never does. He asked me to buy this room before you see... It's not worth it... It's not worth eight hundred and I wouldn't pay a penny less... circular room it is... with no doors or windows... I told him... I said if I buy it... how am I going to get in there... I said if bought a room I'd want to live in it. No good buying rooms you can't use... I wanted to go home... But he wouldn't let go of my peter... You've got to watch these landlords... some of them are dirty bastards.

MARTIN: What, and he had hold of your peter? What was he doing then...

RYDER: Just sitting there holding it that's all... All the time we were talking... wouldn't let go of it.

MARTIN: What – just sitting there holding it... didn't do nothing else then...

RYDER: No... It's funny you know... Another thing about him... it's funny... I always call him HE... But he's a woman really.

MARTIN: A woman?

RYDER: Yes... He's got a beard though... and he wears a man's suit... but I know he's a woman. Funny that isn't it? A woman wearing a beard and a man's suit... It's funny that isn't it? Don't you think that's funny?

MARTIN: How do you know he's a woman... I mean perhaps he's a man?

RYDER: I could tell by his bosom... when I touched him... Got great bosoms he has... And he's got a woman's peter.

Well I mean he ain't got a peter... he's got a woman's one...

MARTIN: You er... You felt it did you... Had a feel did you?

RYDER: Yer... Well I thought... If he's going to hold my peter... I'll hold his... But you couldn't hold his properly you see... Not like he was holding mine... He wouldn't let go... Couldn't get away... I thought how am I going to get away.

MARTIN: Funny business that an' it? Sitting there holding your peter... Huh... I've never had that happen to me... Where did you meet him?

RYDER: Well, I've never met him...

MARTIN: Eh? But... you just been saying that... How could he have done all that if you ain't ever met him?

RYDER: He did it alright. That's why I wouldn't care to meet him. No thank you... I wouldn't want to meet him. Have him sitting there holding my peter all night... No thank you. I'd rather not. I don't go for that sort of thing... I like my privates to be kept private... I don't want no bearded men with great fat bosoms mauling my private bits about... I can't go to sleep some nights wondering about it...

MARTIN: But you ain't met him you said... You said you ain't ever met him. How can he do all that if you ain't ever met him?

RYDER: He can do it at night though can't he? While I'm asleep... I can't do a thing about it when I'm asleep.

MARTIN: Eh?

RYDER: That's why I sit up late... I'm frightened to go to sleep... I'm frightened as soon as I shut my eyes he'll start again. He'll grab my peter and start holding it.

I had to keep waking up last night... Eight times I had
to wake up last night because of him. Every time
I went to sleep... he came and grabbed it...

MARTIN: What in there... In your room? But you said you
ain't never met him...

RYDER: I meet him when I'm asleep. I wouldn't know
about him if I didn't meet him would I... I meet him
when I'm asleep alright. That's why I can't go to sleep...
I went to the police about it... But they wouldn't do
anything... They said they can't do anything about
people you dream about. They said they've got no
control over dreams...

MARTIN: You dream about this... this bloke? Just a dream
is it...

RYDER: Yes... That's why I don't want to go to sleep...
I want to go to sleep see... Because I'm tired... I was up
eight times last night... makes you tired. But I can't go
to sleep. That's why I came in to see you... I keep
dropping off...

MARTIN: It's funny dream to have, ain' it? Very funny
that... that dream. Very funny... Very funny I reckon
that is...

Pause.

MARTIN: You always had it?

RYDER: What?

MARTIN: That dream? You always had that? You been
having it long?

RYDER: What's that got to do with you?

MARTIN: Eh?

RYDER: It's not really any of your business is it? Look
don't start getting inquisitive... That's your trouble you

know... that's what spoils you... You're too bleeding nosey. That's how you got that eye. You want to watch out... some people don't like being cross-examined... I mean who do you think you are... a bloody prosecuting council?

MARTIN: Eh? What are you talking about... I ain't asking you nothing. You told me... You started telling me... all about this dream. You said it...

RYDER: Look why don't you mind your own business? I don't pry into your affairs... I don't keep asking you questions all the time, do I? The way you're going on, you're liable to get another poke in the eye, you know. You want to be careful.

MARTIN: I ain't asked you nothing. I didn't say anything about your dream... you said it.

RYDER: Look – let it drop.

MARTIN: But I ain't.

RYDER: (*Puts the razor to his throat threateningly.*) I said let it drop!!!

MARTIN: Alright... alright...

They sit there silent for a while. RYDER with the razor at MARTIN's throat... looking at him. Finally RYDER speaks.

RYDER: Why do you keep getting at me, eh? You're getting like a bloody policeman, you know... Why must you always be getting at people? That was her trouble... She was like that... she wouldn't mind her own business.

MARTIN: (*Looking up horrified with the razor at his throat.*) What you going to do?

RYDER: What? What do you mean?

MARTIN: Er... well... er... with that there... (*He moves his hand slightly and warily to point at the razor.*) You ain't... you ain't going to cut my throat are you?

RYDER: Eh? What put that idea in your head?

MARTIN: Well... you sitting there like that... an' you...

RYDER: It's not hurting you, is it?

MARTIN: No... but it's...

RYDER: There's no pressure on it... I'm not putting any pressure on it...

MARTIN doesn't answer. He just stares up at RYDER.

RYDER: Don't you like me sitting like this then?

MARTIN: Well, er... No... I, er... mean... I mean... mean...

RYDER: What? What do you mean?

MARTIN: Well... it's uncomfortable...

RYDER: You think I'm going to cut your throat, don't you? Eh? Go on, answer... answer my question... You think I'm going to cut your throat, don't you?

MARTIN: (*Groans.*) I ain't done you no harm, have I? I ain't done nothing to you.

RYDER: Who said you had?

MARTIN: Well, what you wanna cut my throat for?

RYDER: Who said I was going to cut your throat, eh? Who said I'm going to do it?

MARTIN: Well you're sitting there with that... you've got that there an' you... (*Indicates razor again.*)

RYDER: (*Removes the razor from MARTIN's throat and looks at it.*)
What's this? A lot of people have these, you know.
Barbers have these... No harm in having one of these, is
there? It's not criminal to have a razor, is it? That's not a
crime, is it... Just because a barber's got a razor... do you
think he's going to cut your throat then?

MARTIN: You had it on my throat...

RYDER: Well, a barber puts it on your throat, doesn't he?
If a barber was going to shave you... he'd put it on your
throat, wouldn't he?... He'd put it on your throat... like
this... (*He puts the razor back on MARTIN's throat.*) ... and he'd
shave you... like this... (*He starts moving it up and down
MARTIN's chin as though shaving him.*)

MARTIN: (*Squirms.*) Oh... don't... oh... no... oh don't...

RYDER: Keep still... you'll cut yourself. (*He stops the shaving.*)
Blimey, I wouldn't go to your barber's for a shave if
I was you. In your state of nerves... you'd frighten the
life out of him. You'll get yourself cut to pieces. (*He
closes the razor and puts it in his pocket.*) You've got very bad
nerves, haven't you? Have you always had bad nerves?

MARTIN starts moving to get out of bed.

RYDER: Where are you going?

MARTIN: I want to get up.

RYDER: What do you want to get up for?

MARTIN: I just want to get up, that's all.

RYDER: (*Sitting in his way so it is difficult for MARTIN to rise.*)
Why... you must have a reason?

MARTIN: I just want to get up that's all... I'm... I'm tired...
of laying here... And... I want to go to the lavatory. I've
got to go to the lavatory.

RYDER: What – at this time of night?

MARTIN: Well there's no special time is there? I can go anytime... No special time is there... Not for that.

RYDER lets him get up. MARTIN gets out of bed. He is wearing his day clothes.

RYDER: It's out of order.

MARTIN doesn't answer – he walks to the door.

MARTIN: I'll use his backyard. There's a backyard out there. If Ellis won't mend the toilets I'll shit in his backyard!

RYDER: It'll be freezing out there. You'll get a cold up your arse you shit out there.

MARTIN: (*Angry now... in a sort of wild temper.*) It's my arse, an' it... I please myself don't I, eh? You leave me alone that's all. You leave me alone... Or you might get something you've been asking for... I'm not alone, mate... I've got friends, I have... I've got friends, mate... a lot of friends. You might have a gang on you if you ain' careful. I'm not a woman, mate... can't push me around like you can push a woman around. Don't think I didn't see, mate... When I was looking through your keyhole. I saw it... I saw what was going on...

RYDER: Look, you leave my room out of this... What you saw in there is between me and you... no one else.

MARTIN: Eh?

RYDER: You don't want to go around talking about that... You could do yourself a lot of harm you know.

MARTIN: (*Realises he may have said too much.*) Eh... I... (*He starts to back away.*) Don't you touch me now. I ain't going to say nothing.

RYDER: There was nothing to see. You must have imagined it.

MARTIN: Well, there you are... that's why I ain't going to say nothing. That's why I'm not saying nothing.

RYDER: (*Walks towards him.*) Look, I've got a proposition to put to you... You're a smart looking chap... I like the way you handle yourself... You appeal to me. (*Indicates bed.*) Sit down.

MARTIN looks at bed and back at RYDER warily.

MARTIN: Eh?

RYDER: (*Sits on the bed and pats a place beside him.*) Sit down. Come on, no one's going to bite you... I've got a business proposition to put to you.

MARTIN sits down very warily, edging a little way from RYDER.

RYDER: (*Brings out a packet of cigarettes.*) Have a cigarette...

MARTIN takes one and RYDER lights it for him, and his own.

RYDER: I told you I'm in business, didn't I? Well I'm spreading out, you see... I've got to get bigger... I've got to widen my net... and I'm looking for the right sort of chap to come in with me.

MARTIN: What about that job – is it... the one you spoke about...

RYDER: Bigger than that... I'm glad you turned that down... It wouldn't have been your cup of tea. That job wouldn't have been your cup of tea at all... I didn't realise your potential when I offered you that... No... what I'm thinking about, you see... I'm thinking about taking you on the board of directors... with me... make you a partner.

MARTIN: Partner?

RYDER: Yes... what I'll do you see... I'll have to go into this with my accountants, naturally... but what I'll do...

I'll give you so many preference shares... and so many debentures... Of course I can't mention figures now... it needs to be gone into properly. I mean, you can't do a deal like this sitting on a bed... But you're interested, are you?

MARTIN: You're not pulling my leg are you?

RYDER: Well look, I'll tell you what... put your mind at rest... You come to dinner at my place tomorrow night... and you can meet the accountants. They'll put all the figures in front of you.

MARTIN: Yeah? What in your room you mean?

RYDER: Tomorrow night... say eight o'clock? Is that alright for you?

MARTIN: Yes, that's alright for me.

RYDER: You'd better look in your diary first to make sure.

MARTIN: That'll be alright.

RYDER: You'd better check. I don't want you phoning to say can't make it tomorrow... previous appointment or something like that.

MARTIN: I ain't got no previous appointment tomorrow.

RYDER: (*Gets up.*) I'll see you tomorrow then... (*He walks to the window.*)

MARTIN: Where are you going?

RYDER: (*Climbing through.*) Back to my room.

MARTIN: Well, there's the door... (*Points to it.*) Go out here...

RYDER: No, I've got to climb round... my door's bolted on the inside... I don't like leaving the room unfastened... You see, I've got all the day's takings in there. Good night...

He exits. MARTIN looks after him.

MARTIN: (*Mutters.*) Mad... He's bleeding potty... Shit in
the yard! I ain't gonna shit in no yard! Not this time
of night! If the toilets blocked up sod it! It's not my
fault!

He exits his room, and the curtain descends.

ACT THREE

Scene One

Hallway next night. MARTIN leaves his room and crosses over to RYDER's. He knocks on the door and listens, then goes to put his eye to the keyhole, thinks better of it, and listens with ear at door. He knocks once more. RYDER's room is in darkness but his voice is heard speaking through the door.

RYDER: Who is it?

MARTIN: It's me. Martin.

RYDER: Just a minute.

The bolts can be heard being pulled back... about twenty of them. The door opens into RYDER's room and simultaneously the lights rise on the room. The table has a white tablecloth on it, two places have been laid for a meal with silver knives and forks and spoons, two wine glasses one at each place, and a small bottle of wine stands in the middle of the table. RYDER is wearing a very old and tatty dress suit, it is immaculately pressed. MARTIN enters the room and studies the table.

MARTIN: Looks nice, don't it, eh? Looks very nice, don't it?

RYDER: You haven't changed yet.

MARTIN: Eh?

RYDER: You're not dressed.

MARTIN: Not dressed?

RYDER: For dinner... You've not dressed for dinner.

MARTIN: (*Looks at RYDER's dress suit, almost noticing it for the first time.*) Oh... er... you wanted me to put one of them on... the dress suit you mean?

RYDER: Well, naturally, it's going to be very formal tonight, you see.

MARTIN: Well, I didn't know. I mean, you didn't say nothing... not about that. You didn't say to put nothing on...

RYDER: You didn't expect to sit down for dinner dressed like that did you?

MARTIN: Eh? Well you didn't say anything about it being fancy, did you? You said come over and have a bit to eat... You didn't say anything about putting on all them sorts of clothes... you didn't say nothing about that..

RYDER: Well, this is very embarrassing. I thought you had a bit of know how... I mean, you've been around, you're not just out of school, you must have some idea how people behave. Look man, if you're going to be a company director, you've got to learn some table manners, you can't go around eating at people's houses dressed like a tramp. What are you – an eccentric, is that your gimmick. Are you one of those people that go around wearing old clothes and won't stand for the Queen? You can't carry on like that in business, matey... it's alright if you're an artist, doing all that... it's alright then, you can get away with it then, but if you're in business, my old son, you've got to have a bit of decorum.

MARTIN: But I mean I didn't know, you didn't say nothing, did you? I mean, you didn't tell me... I mean, you oughta said.

RYDER: Alright, we don't want to argue about it, you've made a boob. We don't want a lot of excuses. You've made a *faux pas* that's about it... all your old chat isn't going to put that right... The best thing you can do is nip back and put the right clobber on.

MARTIN: Yer, that's all very well an' it... I mean, that's all very well you saying that... But I mean, I ain't got one of them, have I? I mean, I ain't got no call for them sort of clothes, have I... I mean... if you understand my meaning... You see, in my job we don't wear them sort of clothes.

RYDER: You know, if you're going to get on in business, you'll have to have some decent clobber. There's a place down the road, Secondhand High Class Gents' Outfitters... they'll fix you up. Five bob down, half a crown a week, you'll get a marvellous suit down there... He's got some lovely stuff in the window, lightweight stuff, tropical gear, pith helmets too, just the right sort of get-up for the summer.

MARTIN: Yer, I might have a walk down there. I might go down and see him. If I'm going to start picking up some money, might be a good idea to go and see him, pay him a visit... I'll be picking up some money, won't I, on this thing, you know, this proposition we got?

RYDER: If you're the right man.

MARTIN: Yer, that's what I was thinking. I mean I'd need some clothes then alright, wouldn't I? (*He looks at the table again.*) Where's the others?

RYDER: What others?

MARTIN: The accountants. You said the accountants 'd be here.

RYDER: They can't make it. They're tied up with the figures. There's a lot of sorting out to do, you see. Those figures take a lot of going into... You know anything about figures do you?

MARTIN: Yer, I've done a bit. I know they take a lot of going into.

159

RYDER: Yes, there's a lot of work goes into that. They're still working on them now.

MARTIN: Yer, they would be. They would be on them. I know there's a lot goes into it. (*He points at the bottle.*) That wine, is it?

RYDER: Yes. French wine.

MARTIN: Yer, I thought it was, I guessed it was foreign. Good stuff, ain't it?

RYDER: Non vintage, Beojolais, the real stuff.

MARTIN: (*Examining the bottle.*) Yeah?... I thought it'd be a good bit of stuff... I like them foreign wines, you know... I've had 'em before. They're a pretty good drop of stuff they are... most of 'em. (*Examines the cutlery.*) Nice knives and forks they are... Silver, an' they?

RYDER: Hm... Brand new, too... Never been used before. We're the first to eat with them, we are.

MARTIN: Yeah? Really? (*He picks up one of the knives and looks at it.*) Nice too, an' they? Marked... They're marked, an' they? You can tell they're silver alright when they're marked like that.

RYDER: I got then on seven days approval. An advert in the paper it was, so I wrote off for it. I can send them back if I don't like them. Shall we be seated?

MARTIN: What, start, you mean?

RYDER picks up a card near one the plates and reads it.

RYDER: Ah, here's your place. I had them marked, save any confusion. I like doing things properly.

They both sit. RYDER takes up napkin and tucks it in his chin. MARTIN watches him and does the same with his napkin.

MARTIN: I'm sorry about the mistake... you know, not putting on one of them. (*He indicates RYDER's dress suit.*) If you'd let me know earlier like, if you'd told me.

RYDER: I've got one you could borrow if you like? Yes, that's a good idea, you can borrow mine.

MARTIN: What, one of them?

RYDER: Yes, it's a spare one I bought, I never wear it. (*Getting up.*) It doesn't fit me... (*He goes to suitcase and takes out an old and crumpled dress suit.*) Here you are, put this on. I haven't got a shirt or a bow tie, but you can put the coat and trousers on, it'll look much more correct...

MARTIN takes his coat and trousers off, revealing a pair of ragged long pants and a shirt with half the back missing. He puts the dress suit on, it is almost four sizes too big for him.

MARTIN: It's a bit big, an' it... Reckon so... you reckon it's a bit on the big side?

RYDER: It'll be alright... roll the sleeves up... it'll be alright.

MARTIN rolls the sleeves up.

MARTIN: I think I'd better roll the trousers up too... (*He rolls the bottoms of the trousers up and walks back to his seat.*)

RYDER: It suits you. That sort of suit looks good on you.

MARTIN: I feel like one of them lords. I feel a right toff in this.

RYDER: Makes you look something, you know, having that on. You've got the look of someone now.

MARTIN: Have I? Yeah? Really?

He sits down. RYDER opens the wine and pours out the two glasses. He picks up his glass and MARTIN takes his. Then RYDER stands up.

RYDER: (*Turning to picture of the Queen and raising his glass.*)
The Queen!

MARTIN: Oh... (*Bewildered.*) Yer... (*He stands up as well.*)
The Queen.

They toast and both sit down.

MARTIN: Yer they are... Yer... very good.

RYDER: You patriotic?

MARTIN: Who me?... Yer... I was in the services I was...
In the first lot... Yer, I believe in that alright.

RYDER: It's a good thing, patriotism, you know, in
business, helps you get on.

MARTIN: Yer... I always believed in that.

They are both drinking their wine now.

RYDER: She's having another baby you know.

MARTIN: Who, she is?

RYDER: So I've heard.

MARTIN: I ain't heard nothing about that. No ones said
nothing to me, not about that...

RYDER: That's what I heard.

MARTIN: Yer? No one's said nothing to me about it.

RYDER: I was in a cafe, the other day it was, I heard a
couple of soldiers talking about her... they said she was
due for another one.

MARTIN: Yer?

RYDER: They reckoned she was definitely having it.

MARTIN: I ain't heard nothing. No one's said nothing to
me, not about that they ain't.

RYDER: Well, that's what they reckon, she's going to have it alright. Well, she's going in for a family isn't she? I mean you can see that, her and him. (*He looks at the picture.*)

MARTIN: Yer, I reckon so. Still, I ain't heard nothing, not about any new one.

RYDER: Well, that's what they were saying.

Pause.

RYDER: They get on well you know, those two.

MARTIN: Yer, well you always see 'em out together. If you see her, he's always with her nearly.

RYDER: Yes. I forgot to send her a card. I only remembered the other day.

MARTIN: Eh?

RYDER: I always send her a Xmas card, and him. I always send him one too, but I forgot it this year.

MARTIN: Do you? What every year?

RYDER: Yes, ever since my mother died.

MARTIN: I've never sent her one.

RYDER: I used to send one to her mother as well you know, when she was Queen... I think it's right, I think we ought to. I mean at Xmas, that's when the Queen of Heaven had her baby, I mean that's what it's for, Xmas, isn't it... a baby, the son of God, I mean that's the idea of Xmas. That's why I send it. I think we all ought to send the Queen a card on that day... everyone, they all ought to send a card.

MARTIN: (*Pours himself another drink.*) Yer, well I'm with that, I'm a Christian... I support that alright. I think that's what I'll do next year, I'll send her a card. Buckingham Palace, an' it, that's the address?

RYDER: Do you like onion soup?

MARTIN: Yer, I like that, yer, that'll be nice.

RYDER takes a tin out of a pot on the stove and pours half of the contents onto MARTIN's plate, and the other half onto his own. He then gets a wrapped loaf and puts it on the table.

RYDER: Eight day bread... Do you like that? It keeps for eight days that does... doesn't go dry, in fact it wouldn't go dry if you kept it for eight weeks, just get damper and damper. That's what grease-proof wrapping is for... it keeps the water in...

MARTIN: Marvellous an' it, what they can do these days. (*He tears into the bread and starts wolfing the bread and soup.*) Hm... nice drop of soup this is.

RYDER: I had some meat the other day, four years old it was. Deep freeze stuff, they keep it for years in those ice boxes. (*He picks up the loaf, looks at it, puts it down again.*) Malnutrition in hermetically sealed bags. Frozen peas and the H bomb, that's the menu for this century.

Pause during which MARTIN wolfs away hungrily.

RYDER: You know when that bomb goes off there's going to be a big bang.

MARTIN: Yer I reckon it is.

RYDER: It'll be a bang alright. We'll all go up you know.

MARTIN: (*Wiping his plate clean with bread.*) Yer... I reckon your right there. You ain't ate your soup.

RYDER: What a bleeding bang there's going to be.

MARTIN: Don't you want that soup?

RYDER: Hm? (*He looks at his plate.*) No...

MARTIN takes it and starts to wolf into it, with more bread.

RYDER: I'm not bothered you know...

MARTIN: Eh?

RYDER: About the bomb. It doesn't bother me.

MARTIN: (*Pouring another drink.*) That's what I say... What
I say, if they drop it they drop it. What's got to be's got
to be. No good making a fuss about it, eh? Get down the
tube, that's the best place. Piccadilly, that's the one, that's
the deepest. I went down there during the last lot. Nice
and warm down there is was, I used to like it down there.
'Cos soon as the war ended they made us come up...
wouldn't let us sleep down there anymore... Them
bloody porters, pigs they are, they're pigs you know,
all of 'em...

RYDER goes over to the oven, opens it and takes out a kind of pie.

RYDER: (*Looking at open oven.*) That's the best place you
know...

MARTIN: What?

RYDER: In there. Get your head in there. You'd be alright
then. A bobsworth of gas. I reckon a bob would do it...
Don't you reckon so... Shilling single for a nice trip...
there you are, a day excursion to Heaven, all for a bob.
Where else can you travel as cheap as that?

MARTIN: Eh? What you mean... do yourself in...? No,
I'd sooner go down the tube, mate. You'd be alright
down there, take my word, you'd be safe and sound
down there.

RYDER: (*Puts the pie on the table.*) Do you want any of this
pie? I made it myself.

MARTIN: (*Eagerly.*) Yer... I wouldn't mind some of that.

RYDER: You can have it all if you like, I'm not hungry.

MARTIN: (*Grabs the pie and starts wolfing into it.*) Hm...
   (*With his mouth full.*) Nice this... It's alright... ain't got
   no vegetables, I s'pose, have you?

RYDER: What do you think this is, a bleeding hotel?

MARTIN: Eh?

RYDER: Don't get greedy... you don't want to get greedy,
   you know.

MARTIN: No, I ain't... You said come to dinner, I thought
   there might be some vegetables, that's all... vegetables
   is dinner, an' it... But it's alright, if you ain't got any,
   I mean if you ain't got any, it's alright... I'll fill up with
   bread, the bread'll do me... (*He starts tearing into the bread
   again.*)

RYDER: (*Watches him eat for a while.*) You're a bit of a pig
   on the quiet, aren't you? A bit of a gutsy... I've been
   watching you eat, you're a right guts, you are, aren't
   you? Got no bloody refinement, have you?

MARTIN: (*With his mouth full.*) Don't you start taking the piss
   out of me, mate. I ain't no pig, I'm a human being, mate,
   I'm human, I am... You want to be careful what you're
   calling me now, I got something on you, you want to
   watch out.

RYDER: Don't start threatening me. You don't want to
   threaten me, you know.

MARTIN: I can threaten alright, mate. I can threaten,
   you don't want to worry about that... I saw what was
   going on through that keyhole. I ain't forgotten that
   either, so watch out... (*He indicates his bandaged eye.*)

RYDER: You're too touchy, you know, that's your trouble.
   You've got too many inhibitions, that's what's wrong
   with you.

MARTIN: Yer, well I know a few things that's wrong with you, too. You're off your nut, mate, that's what's wrong with you. I seen you through that keyhole, don't worry, I'm on to you. I've seen what you were doing to Sophie, and coming in my room with that razor, putting that razor on my throat, I could have you for that...

RYDER: Sophie's in Manchester.

MARTIN: That's what you say, I bet she ain't though. I bet she ain't in no Manchester. An' those photographs... (*He points to them.*) ... I s'pose that ain't looney either, eh... cutting up them photographs... you looked looney alright doing that.

RYDER gets up.

MARTIN: (*Backing to door.*) Don't you touch me... don't you lay no finger on me, you want to pack that in mate, you don't want to start nothing like that.

RYDER: (*Advancing on him.*) What have I supposed to have done to Sophie, then, eh? What are you trying to say I've done then, eh?

MARTIN: I ain't saying you done nothing, mate. I ain't saying you done nothing to her. What you done to her, that's your affair, that's between you and her, I ain't bothered about that... All I'm saying, don't start nothing with me...

MARTIN makes a dive at the door, but RYDER gets there first, and stands with his back to it facing MARTIN. MARTIN backs away.

MARTIN: Look – you don't want to start nothing with me, mate... I'm your partner an' I? We're in business, ain't we? We're doing a deal, we don't want no bother, do we... not between us... we're chinas, ain't we, me and you, we got this big deal. We don't want to fall out over her, over that old bag. What she got, mate, you ask me... what she got, she deserved it. I reckon she asked for it... she had it coming to her, her and that Ellis they've been asking for it. Her coming in our room like she did, mucking about with you, I reckon that's asking for it alright, you ask me, that's asking for it alright...

RYDER: She's not been in my room.

MARTIN: That's what I say. I mean if she had, that's what I mean. If she had been in here. It'd serve her right, wouldn't it? They've pushed me around, them two you know. They ain't done no good for me... Not like you, you've been a friend, you've helped me.

The dogs start howling, very mournful. They both listen.

MARTIN: Them dogs sound uneasy, don't they, tonight... I reckon they're pining. They do pine, don't they, dogs? They've been like that on and off the last two days... ever since Sophie went. I suppose they miss her.

RYDER: They've still got Ellis. He's still down there.

MARTIN: Yer... She used to help feed 'em though. See, time he gets round to them all, it's time to start feeding 'em again... So many of 'em you see. She used to help him. Besides, he's out a lot looking for more, see, he's always out collecting. They ain't getting looked after properly. Unnatural that, ain't it? The way he likes dogs, he can't get enough of 'em, he can't.

The dogs continue to howl for a while.

RYDER: He's unkind to those animals.

MARTIN: Who, Ellis? No, he's not unkind to 'em. Not to dogs, he ain't... it's the only thing he likes...

RYDER: He's got all those dogs in a little rabbit hutch... they're crammed in there they are. I went down and had

a peep the other day, he's got some of them three in a
hutch... they can't move.

MARTIN: He's not unkind to 'em though... He thinks the
world of them dogs.

RYDER: He's a swine, a dirty swine. I saw him after I had
a look in the cellar, as he was coming out. Sitting in that
rocking chair he was, asleep... his head back snoring...
I felt like slitting his throat. The dirty black git. Indian
isn't he?

MARTIN: Yer... off the boats. He come off the boats...
Laskar, that's what he is. Used to sell ties... That's how
he got this house, selling ties...

Pause.

MARTIN: Er... this business deal. We going to do it then?..
Me and you... we going to join up are we? We could
make a bit of money between us you know, me and you.
I mean I got ideas, I've got ideas for things. We work
right, we could have a house like this in no time... Me
and you working together, we could get a place like
this. All them handbags, I mean we could sell all them
handbags for a start... You could always get more, can't
you?... I mean when they've gone, you can put your
hands on some more, I s'pose?

RYDER: Yes. I've got contacts...

MARTIN: Tell you another idea... Another idea I got. Get
a fiddle, that's what I'd like to do... If I can get me hands
on a fiddle, you can make money out of one of them.
I know a bloke that had a fiddle, he used to play in the
West End... In Piccadilly Arcade, that's where he used
to play. You get in there, in Piccadilly Arcade, you can
make twelve bob a day with a fiddle. They're easy to
learn too... nothing in 'em so they say... And you don't
pay no tax, you don't keep any books see... That's where
you go wrong I reckon... keeping books... That's where

I reckon I could help you, give you some of them
wrinkles see... That's where I could fit in good...

RYDER: Well, that's why I picked you. I knew you had
a flair for that sort of thing. As soon as I saw you,
I thought to myself, here's a chap that's got it... here's a
fellow with know-how, I could see it, man... I could see
you were executive potential... Top class material, it
stands out.

MARTIN: I've been around. See, look, I ain't got no
degrees or nothing like that. I ain't been to none of
them colleges or nothing. I ain't saying I'm educated,
not like you are, or... you know... I ain't saying that.

RYDER: You've got a natural flair. I'm not looking for high
school boys. These college boys, what do they know?

MARTIN: That's it, ain't it? I mean that's what I say. It's
like this man, I mean this is the point... the point is this,
I mean I ain't ever had no chance... I mean that's the gist
of it...

Pause.

MARTIN: We going to do it then? Me and you... We going
to sign up?

RYDER: It's a proposition.

MARTIN: Yer, well that's what I say... It's definitely a
proposition an' it? I mean we've only got to draw up
the papers... that's all we got to do...

RYDER: How much capital could you put in?

MARTIN: Eh? Well, erm... not money. I ain't got no money.

RYDER: Well, I mean you can't really expect to get in
without capital, can you? I mean unless you've got
some assets? Have you got any hidden assets?

MARTIN: Well, I ain't got no money, that's the trouble... That's been the trouble before, on other deals... that's happened before...

RYDER: What about your bank manager? How do you stand with him?

MARTIN: Well, I ain't got no bank, you see... I mean, not having any money, you see, I ain't ever bothered.

Pause.

MARTIN: I could work on percentage, how about that? That'd be alright wouldn't it? If I worked on percentage, I mean you'd still be the gov'nor, I'd be under your orders... I'd take orders...

RYDER: We'll see... finish your dinner first, and we'll see. There might be a solution.

MARTIN: Yer, that's it. That might be it. (*He sits down and starts on the pie again. He starts to wolf it, looks at RYDER, and tries to eat more daintily.*)

RYDER: If I formed you into a company, and bought you out, as a loss, a loss company to write off taxes... That might work out.

MARTIN: Yer, that's it, that's the way...

RYDER: Do you like that... do you like that pie?

MARTIN: Yer, it's good. It's tasty, very tasty... got a nice taste it 'as... How do you make it?

RYDER: Quite simple. All you need is some flour and water and a tin of kitty Kat.

MARTIN: Yer, I s'pose... eh? What did you say it was?

RYDER: Kitty Kat.

MARTIN: Kitty... cat food...

RYDER: It's alright, quite fresh... You know there's more vitamins in a tin of that than a pound of steak.

MARTIN: You rotten sod... (*He stumbles up.*) You done that on purpose... invite me in here... and give me bleeding cat food...

RYDER: Well, what do you expect... fillet steak?

MARTIN groans and makes for the door.

RYDER: Where are you going?

MARTIN answers with another groan and exits... RYDER goes to door and shouts after him.

RYDER: It's out of order!

Blackout.

Scene Two

RYDER's room the same evening a little while later. MARTIN sits on the chair, watching RYDER, who is sitting on the bed carving at the table with his razor. They are both wearing dress suits still.

MARTIN: (*Watching RYDER for a while.*) What you, er... What you keep that razor for?

RYDER: Cutting things... and shaving.

MARTIN: That'll be no good for shaving... spoils a razor doing that... makes 'em blunt.

RYDER: I've got a strop...

MARTIN: What for – sharpening it?

Pause.

MARTIN: That all you use it for... shaving?

RYDER: And cutting.

Pause.

MARTIN: That's what them girls were killed with...
a razor... had their throats cut with one of them.

RYDER: (*Still very preoccupied with what he is doing.*) They're
good for that... they're very good for that, these are...
You could cut a throat easy with one of these.

MARTIN: Yer...

Pause.

MARTIN: They ain't caught him yet... They reckon it's
someone round this area... They reckon he's living
round here.

Pause.

MARTIN: They ain't found no clues though... not nothing
they ain't found. I mean they sometimes find some
clothes or something... you always read it in the papers
when they've found something – the police I mean.
I was reading the other day, where they found a raincoat,
sounded a good one it did... one of them with a big fur
collar it was.

Pause.

MARTIN: I wonder what they do with all them clothes
they find, I mean them clothes that all these
murderers an' that wear... 'Cos there always topping
some down, an' they... some murderer... I mean they've
got to do something with all them clothes, an' they... they
don't want 'em piling up down there, do they?
I went down there one day, to Brixton, they was topping
some bloke down there, a car dealer he was. I mean them
blokes, car dealers I mean, they make some good money
don't they? I thought, I bet he'd have a bit of good
clobber on him , a bloke like that. A big crowd there
was, down there, shouting and that... and some woman,
she was screaming out and banging on the gate. They
didn't want this bloke topped it turned out... Protesting

173

they was. I thought it was his family at first. But they wasn't relations or nothing like that at all, didn't even know him, most of 'em... making a lot of fuss though, they was... Funny that, ain't it? Funny that, I thought, there's all of us standing out here, an' there's him in there going to be topped an' all these people shouting an' hollering, they ain't going to do him no good I thought. I mean the law ain't going to stop hanging him, just 'cos there's some people outside banging on the gate. Soon as he was done like, they all went home, packed up their banners and went home...

Pause.

MARTIN: I never found out about the clobber. What they do with it, I mean...

Pause.

MARTIN: You've got some fair old clobber ain't you, yourself. I mean that dress suit, an' this one here... (*He rises and walks to the cupboard.*) You got any more in here...

RYDER springs up and stops him going to the cupboard.

RYDER: Leave that alone.

MARTIN: I was only going to have a look to see if you had any clobber in there.

RYDER: That's personal. What's in there is personal.

MARTIN: 'At's alright... I wasn't going to touch it... I was only going to have a little peep, see if you had any clobber in there... But I won't touch it, mate, not if it's personal. (*He walks away from the cupboard, and sits on the chair.*)

MARTIN: They had no right, you know, bringing this chair in here... They took it while I was out... They wouldn't come in and take it while I was still in there... they wait till you've gone out...

Pause.

MARTIN: I got to come in here now, if I want to sit on my own chair. I've got to come in here. In your room.

RYDER: You can have it back.

MARTIN: Eh?

RYDER: You can have it back if you want it.

MARTIN: What will they say... Ellis and her... if she comes back...

RYDER: They can't say anything, it's your chair.

MARTIN: Yer, I know. It's my chair, it's my chair alright. It's out of my room that is. But if I take it back, what are they going to say... they might cut up nasty, I mean after them putting it in here, they might cut up nasty if I take it back and put it in there.

RYDER: I don't need it anymore. It's no good to me now, that chair.

MARTIN: No good... what are you going to sit on then?

RYDER: I'm going. I won't be here after tonight. That's why I had that dinner, sort of last supper.

Pause.

MARTIN: You taking that other room then... That circular one, that you had a dream about?

RYDER: No, I'm finishing with rooms, mate. They can keep their rooms, their dirty crap holes. I've had enough. I'm getting out of this madhouse.

MARTIN: We get them handbags sold, we could get a good house, me and you. We could get a place. A good place... you know what I mean... with a lot of rooms... let 'em off... we'd be set up. We could have the downstairs, 'stead

175

of being up here, mate... we could be downstairs... be like Ellis... with all the downstairs, and rents... a lot of rents coming in... Be a good set-up that... Eh? What about it? Eh?

RYDER: I've got other plans... I've made other plans...

MARTIN: What about the bags though... We've got to sell the bags first though, ain't we?

RYDER: I saw my mother last night... She looked just the same as when I was a little boy. It was in that room, I was talking to this landlord, and she came in... Well it was her, you see I was talking to this landlord, and he'd just got hold of my peter and... I was going to tell him to stop. I was just going to tell him to stop, and then... I saw it was my mother... She asked me where I'd been... why I hadn't been home...

MARTIN: What, in a dream was it?

Pause.

RYDER: Eh?

MARTIN: In that dream, was it... that dream you have?

RYDER: (*Looks at him.*) Do you believe in spiritualism?

MARTIN: What... ghosts you mean?

RYDER: This was no ghost... it was my mother. She said she had a room for me, a good room. Said she'd been keeping it for me... and she said she can't find my dad... and she wanted to know why I hadn't been home... Our house was bombed, I told her... It's not there anymore, it was bombed... first year of the war it was... a stray bomber they said... he only had one bomb and he dropped it on our house. My mum and dad were in it... together they were, in the bedroom, that's where they found them... He ought to be with her... but she said she can't find him.

Pause.

RYDER: She kept asking why I didn't come home... She said my room's been done up... She's done it up nice, she said... and she wants me to go home and help her find my dad...

MARTIN: That's a funny dream, that... a very funny dream that is... I've never had a dream like that... Only dream I ever had...

RYDER: It wasn't a dream... It was no dream, mate... She was standing there... She had those clothes on, the one's she was wearing... before I went to school, I remember she had them on... She waved to me as I ran up the street, I remember those clothes alright. I wouldn't forget them...

Pause.

RYDER: The teacher came in and told me, she said your house has been blown up... she wouldn't let me go home... she wouldn't let me go home to my dinner... I had to stay in the school... They wouldn't let me go home... I'm going home now though... They can't stop me now... I'm going to help my mother see if she can find my dad... (*He gets up off the bed.*) Yes, that's what I'm going to do... I've got my plans, my plans are made...

MARTIN: What about them bags then? We've got to sell them bags first.

RYDER: I haven't got time for that... I haven't got time for that now... I've got this other thing to do... I've got these other plans.

MARTIN: What about this deal then? We was going to do a deal... We got this deal to do first, ain't we? You was going to turn me into a company, for taxes you said, write off taxes... you remember... You ain't forgot that, have you?

Pause.

MARTIN: I mean you can't back out of a deal, can you?

Pause.

MARTIN: You're not backing out, are you?

Pause.

MARTIN: Sell them bags first... we sell them bags first and I'll give you a hand... we can go and find your dad together... both of us... Yer, that's the best way... Have two of us looking... better'n one...

RYDER: I've got to go.

MARTIN: Wait to sell the bags first, eh? That's the best idea... If you have another dream... If you have that dream tonight... see, you could tell her, tell your mum, we got to sell these bags first and then we can both give her a hand... Eh? What about that? Do it that way, eh?

RYDER: You're not getting my meaning... You're not getting it at all are you? You're not with me... You see, where I'm going, where I've got to go, you can't come with me... It's just me they want... they're waiting... they've been waiting a long time... I know they want me... I've known for a long time... you see, I'm a mystic, I'm too mystical that's my trouble, I can sense these things... I can tell by the feel of things... It's tonight I've got to go. I've got to go and tell them all my sins. I couldn't help what I've done... I didn't mean to do all the things I've done... I hope they understand that... I hope they understand that when I tell them... When they make a judgement... I hope they take things into consideration...

Long pause.

MARTIN: What about the bags... I s'pose you're taking all them, are you? All this gear is being taken, I s'pose... is it? I s'pose you're taking all that?

Pause.

MARTIN: It'll be heavy... carrying all this gear about...
be heavy you know...

Pause.

MARTIN: Tell you what, here's an idea... leave it, leave it
all here... while you're gone, I'll run the business... That's
a way of doing it, an' it? That's a good way to do it...
I'll sell all them bags... I'll get a good price for them...
I'll get a top price... I'm a partner an' I... I've got a share
in 'em... You gave me a share in 'em... You don't want to
forget that...

RYDER just sits now and stares in front of him.

MARTIN: Eh? What do you think of that... If I sell 'em...
If I run the business, eh? (*He goes up close and shakes
RYDER.*) Eh? What do you think, man? Eh?... That's
the way to do it, an' it... that's the way...

RYDER: I didn't mean to do that to Sophie... I hope
they'll understand... when they pass the judgement
I hope they'll understand that... It should be taken
into consideration.

MARTIN: Look, we're not talking about that man, it's
the gear, it's the gear we're talking about... all this
clobber and the bags... You're going to leave 'em
ain'tcha?

RYDER: You're patriotic aren't you?

MARTIN: Yer, like I told you... I support that mate...
I support the Royalty. I could get a good price on
them bags... If I had them bags... I could get started
big on them...

RYDER: (*Points to picture of the Queen.*) That picture... you can
have it... It's yours.

MARTIN: (*Looks at it.*) Oh... Yer... Thanks... That's nice... Er... that's the sort of thing you could carry... you could carry that easy... but them bags... They're going to be difficult.

RYDER: Piss off.

MARTIN: Eh?

RYDER: Piss off.

MARTIN: Eh? What do you mean?

RYDER: You getting deaf? Your ears packing up are they? You going mutton?

MARTIN: No, I just... eh... what's the matter?

RYDER: The party's over see... the dance has ended... Get my meaning... So piss off...

He walks towards MARTIN who backs out. RYDER walks to the door and watches MARTIN cross the corridor and enter his room. He shouts after him.

RYDER: Poke your bleeding nose in my room any more and I'll cut it off.

He closes his door quietly and tip-toes down the stairs. MARTIN's door opens quietly and he watches him. As soon as RYDER has gone, MARTIN tip-toes over to his room and enters it. He picks up the case full of handbags, looks all round the room to see what else he might take as well... His eyes light on the cupboard. He opens the door to reveal SOPHIE completely bald, bound and gagged.

MARTIN: (*Steps back.*) Blimey...

Curtain.

Scene three

Hallway. MARTIN can be heard coming up the stairs. He is still wearing the borrowed dress suit. RYDER's room is in darkness. Only the hallway is lit.

MARTIN: Up here... Here it is... up here... this is where he lives.

He appears at the top of the stairs, followed by TWO POLICEMEN in raincoats. They walk towards RYDER's room.

MARTIN: Here you are, in here... that's his room, in there. That's where he lives.

One of the POLICEMEN tries the door which is bolted. SOPHIA appears at the top of the stairs.

SOPHIA: You got him? Is he there? (*She approaches the men.*) He's in there, an' he? The sod... is he in there?

1st POLICEMAN: (*Tries the door again.*) It's locked. The door's locked.

MARTIN: Bolted it is... on the inside... He bolts it. Got lots of bolts in there, he 'as... on the inside.

2nd POLICEMAN: (*Knocks on door.*) Open up. Hullo... You in there... open up... open this door... I'm a Police Officer. (*He listens but there is no reply.*)

MARTIN: Break it in... That's the way to get him out, mate... break it in... break the door in...

1st POLICEMAN: Whose house is this?

SOPHIA: It's alright, you can smash it in. It's my house... It belongs to me and Ellis... You can break it down.

MARTIN: You want to hurry up mate... he might be out that bleeding window... He can get out that window in there...

SOPHIA: Don't let him get away... Smash the door in...
Don't let him get away, the bloody bastard! Look what
he's done to my hair... Look, the bleeding sod... He's cut
it all off... look... I'll cut him open when I get my hands
on him.

MARTIN: Bleeding murderer he is... You want to smash that
door down... get him out... he's got to be topped he has...
He's killed all them girls, he 'as. He's the one that's
killed all them girls... That's where he gets the handbags
from... Bloody madman, he is...

1st POLICEMAN: He's not the one that's been killing the
girls. He's not guilty of that.

MARTIN: Eh? What you talking about, ain't guilty? 'Cos
he's guilty, he's the one alright... Look what he done
to my eye... stuck a bleeding cane in it... I almost lost
that eye...

1st POLICEMAN: We've got him down the station... the
one that's been doing the murders... He was arrested this
morning. He's made a full confession.

SOPHIA: No, it's him... he's the one... Look what he done
to my hair... Locked me in a cupboard he did... tied up
I was. Three days he kept me in there... All he gave me
was two pies to eat...

MARTIN: Kitty Kat... That's what they was. He made me
eat some... bleeding cat food. He wants doing in, he does.

SOPHIA: I'd do him in... If I got my hands on him... I'd do
him in.

MARTIN: He's the one that's been doing the murders mate,
I seen him... He's the one alright...

2nd POLICEMAN: We've got him down the station. The
chap that's been doing the murders is under arrest.

1st POLICEMAN: We got him this morning, early. Caught red-handed he was... Constable saw him running away from the girl.

2nd POLICEMAN: He's confessed. Full confession in triplicate, signed and witnessed.

SOPHIA: I bet he's the one... you've got the wrong one down there... He's the one alright... him in there.

MARTIN: I seen him... I seen him with his razor.

SOPHIA: I seen him too.

1st POLICEMAN: Stand back...

SOPHIA and MARTIN move back out of the way. The POLICEMAN knocks on the door again.

1st POLICEMAN: Can you hear me? I'm a Police Officer... I want you to open this door... Hullo... Can you hear me?

MARTIN: He can hear you alright... He ain't going to open that door though, mate... He ain't going to open up for you... He knows what he's got coming...

SOPHIA: Smash it in... break it down.

1st POLICEMAN: Out of the way...

2nd POLICEMAN: Stand back!

They both charge at the door, which for all RYDER's bolts is not very substantial at all and soon caves in. They all crowd into the room. RYDER is lying there with his head in the gas oven. One of the POLICEMEN breaks the window, while the other turns the gas off.

1st POLICEMAN: (*Examining RYDER.*) He's a goner!

MARTIN: He's gone? (*Running across to where the handbags are and trying to scoop them all up.*) He's left the bags! These are mine! These bags are mine! I'm his partner!

SOPHIA: The bastard! He's topped himself!
(*To POLICEMEN.*) Look what he's done to me,
an' he's got away with it, the swine!

She tries to kick the body. The POLICEMEN prevent her.

SOPHIA: Let me go! I'll give him what for! (*She kicks out at the body.*)

MARTIN: These bags are mine! They belong to me!

1st POLICEMAN: (*To SOPHIA, struggling with her as she tries to kick the body.*) It wasn't him! We've got the murderer!

SOPHIA: Don't tell me who it wasn't! I know who it was cut my hair off and locked me in the bleeding cupboard! The bastard!

MARTIN: These are my bags, eh? Alright?

Curtain.